THIS IS THE ONLY WAY TO SOLVE THE IMMIGRATION "PROBLEM":

THE RADICAL HUMAN RIGHTS APPROACH THAT CAN BREAK THE LEFT-RIGHT STALEMATE

ANIS SHIVANI

FUturist Press
Houston, Boston, Los Angeles

ii

Requests for permission to reproduce selections from this book should be directed to: Permissions Department, FUturist Press, 2041 Norfolk Street, Houston, Texas 77098, or FUturist.Press@gmail.com.

Published in the United States by FUturist Press, Houston, Texas 77098

LIBRARY OF CONGRESS CATALOGING-IN-PUBLICATION DATA

This Is the Only Way to Solve the Immigration "Problem": The Radical Human Rights Approach That Can Break the Left-Right Stalemate / Anis Shivani, 1st ed.
ISBN: 978-1976255540
1. Immigration—Political Aspects—United States. 2. Donald J. Trump—Immigration Policies—United States. 3. Dreamers—United States—2001-. 4. Immigration Reform—United States—1965-. 5. Immigration Law—United States—1882-.

Composition by FU-fu!
This book was set in Perpetua

Printed in the United States of America

2 4 6 8 9 7 5 3 1

FUturist Press: A Coalition for Millennial Change publishes fine books of elegantly-written polemics, aesthetic statements, philosophical investigations, moral and cultural criticism, and imaginative writing driven by eclectic, personal, idiosyncratic knowledge of the humanist disciplines; we seek to change the discourse around politics, literature, and art by discovering ideas that have yet to take shape, not regurgitate the ones already known and understood. Stay tuned for our future offerings!

By the Same Author

Anatolia and Other Stories
The Fifth Lash and Other Stories
Karachi Raj: A Novel
A History of the Cat in Nine Chapters or Less: A Novel

My Tranquil War and Other Poems
Whatever Speaks on Behalf of Hashish: Poems
Soraya: Sonnets
The Moon Blooms in Occupied Hours: Poems
Confessions I: Poems

Against the Workshop: Provocations, Polemics, Controversies
Literary Writing in the Twenty-First Century: Conversations

Why Did Trump Win? Charting the Stages of Neoliberal Reactionism During America's Most Turbulent Election Cycle
Confronting American Fascism: Essays on the Democratic Collapse, 2001-2017

For Those Who Refuse to Compromise on Human Rights for All Persons vi

Contents

Acknowledgments

My deep thanks to Andrew O'Hehir of *Salon* for publishing my work. My thanks also to Don Hazen at *AlterNet*, Rob Kall at *OpEd News*, and Michael Woodson at KPFT Houston for their support and promotion. I am deeply grateful to John S.W. Park, Kevin R. Johnson, and David Brotherton, who are among those from whom I learned everything I know about immigration: those are the true experts! My thanks also to Ali Eteraz and Harvey Hix for their consistent encouragement, and to Peter Schey and Yvonne Koopman for years of assistance. Thanks to Benjamin Rybeck, Mark Haber, Dustin Pickering, Nancy Wozny, Matt Riley, Chris Wise, Fran Sanders, Dean Liscum, Betsy Huete, Rahul Mitra, Gemini Wahhaj, Elora Shehabuddin, Fady Joudah, James Adams, Elina Petrova, Dom Zuccone, Mike Alexander, Dave Cowen, Laura Pena, Gary Rosin, Chuck and Mary Wemple, Amir Safi, Gerald Cedillo, Stalina Villarreal, Kathy Fay, Stephen Gros, Jessica Biano, Winston Derden, Doni Wilson, Elizabeth White-Olsen, Holly Walrath, Layla al-Bedawi, Robert Clark, Buckey Rea, Mike McGuire, Saba Husain, Karen Hyde Abercrombie, Emelia Forbau, Aliah Lavonne Tigh, and Dee Dillman in Houston. Thanks to Brazos Bookstore for being the best independent bookstore on either side of the Mississippi, and to all the staff there for always being such gracious hosts for my book launches. Of course, my deepest appreciation to Mehnaaz Momen, who is a scholar of immigration and citizenship in her own right, and who has experienced many of the realities and contingencies described in this book, as an immigrant, as a teacher, and as an activist—as have I.

Cover Art: F. Childe Hassam, *Avenue of the Allies: Brazil, Belgium* 1918, Oil on canvas, 36 5/16 x 24 5/16 in.
Courtesy Los Angeles County Museum of Art

Ten Things Americans Don't Understand About Our Immigration System

"There were other immigrants who came here in the bottom of slave ships, who worked even longer, even harder, for less, but they too had a dream that one day their sons, daughters, grandsons, granddaughters, great grandsons, great granddaughters might pursue prosperity and happiness in this land." — HUD Secretary Ben Carson, March 6, 2017

The immigration debate has become mired in myths, falsehoods, and half-truths, with little clarity amongst liberals or conservatives alike. Conservatives think there's nothing wrong with Trump defending America to keep "the bad ones" out, because, after all, every sovereign nation should have that right. Liberals concede the point, but modify it a bit by claiming exception for the "good ones," such as the "Dreamers" (those who were "brought" here at a young age "due to no fault of their own"). Immigrant rights advocates seek an elusive middle ground, even as the terrain of immigration has shifted from morality or economics or even national identity, to the spectacle of crime and punishment.

Most Americans who do not have direct experience with the immigration system are easily misled by the claims of the xenophobes, which sound commonsensical, such as the (false) notion that immigrants drive down wages and make natives lose their jobs. They may not want to go to the extreme of taking up arms to defend the nation—as do the Minutemen on the southwestern border—but they passively accept the myths. What many don't realize is that each time a right is taken away from immigrants, with implied consent, it eventually affects citizens' rights too. To remain distant from the issue is no longer an option for any of us. Ben Carson's comment above had less to do with our past history with slavery than our future ideal for immigrants.

We want to shut ourselves up behind the Wall—paid for by Mexico, of course—as we turn citizenship into a privilege derived from exaggerated notions of loyalty. Such self-disciplining consciousness is the other side of the overt criminalization of immigrants. American citizenship has become the sole passage to a utopia of freedom by way of crushing the undeserving other, the poor immigrant.

What is going on? Why has the country turned so anti-immigrant (despite hollow claims from politicians that we remain "a nation of immigrants")? Did 9/11 cause this? Is it because of Trump? Or is there something predating terrorism or the authoritarian upsurge? Is changing sentiment toward immigrants rooted in rational anxieties, such as concern about jobs, or does it represent a free-floating pessimistic discourse that is as much a part of our self-construction as the optimism we're more used to hearing?

Here, then, are some of our most damaging misunderstandings in this defining area of national policy:

1. There is no line to get into.

Americans seem to think that if you are a capable person somewhere in the world, you just need to get in line and if everything checks out you're in. Or if you have relatives who have spent their life in America and you want to join them, you can join the line. The idea that people should "get in the back of the line," a mantra we hear every time so-called comprehensive immigration reform (CIR) comes up, doubles down on the nonsense. There is no line, only a nightmarish engagement with an immigration bureaucracy for those lucky enough to deal with it.

Perhaps there is a theoretical line. If you are a sibling of a Filipino citizen, you may wait up to twenty years to get in—if your family member will take full financial responsibility, at the risk of being pursued in court if an emergency compels you to seek public assistance. If you are a high-skilled immigrant in demand by Silicon Valley, you may seek an H1-B visa. But you must be the type of person who fits corporate America's vision of a good citizen in every aspect of your life. Immigrants with technical skills arrive on a presumed pathway to citizenship, even if theoretically they are temporary immigrants.

What if you are a bright young person on a visitor visa, but want to study and live in the U.S.? Adjusting your status may not be easy, and if you run afoul of any technicalities, you're out of luck and "illegal."

What if your visa has lapsed, yet you found the resources to establish a life here, marrying a citizen and having children? Can you correct your status? You'd have to prove hardship of a kind that would satisfy the immigration bureaucracy, a fantasy of torture and devastation for yourself and your family, rather than any realistic definition of hardship.

The line is a fantasy. For those corporate America desires, they go straight to the front anyway, their papers awaiting them and their families. For those who have ever struggled in life, who may be from poor backgrounds but want to better themselves through education and civic participation, the options are limited.

Many of us know someone who may be an outstanding citizen in every respect, even a prominent member of the community, except for the lack of technical legality. They may even have the money to pursue a legal avenue. Have we ever considered why these people choose to remain "illegal?" If there were a line for accomplished immigrants who desire to fix their status, wouldn't they join in?

Shouldn't the immigrant, without having to be tied to an absurd mythology of hardship, be able to fulfill the desire to stay, based on equities built up which would be lost with the finality of deportation? Isn't that what most people imagine when they say that those who want to stay should "get right with the law," that they should pay the fines and "get their citizenship?" But our immigration practices have become so distorted that such possibilities do not really exist.

2. The legal/illegal distinction is meaningless.

Both restrictionists and reformists love to say, "I'm for legal immigration, but against illegal immigration." The current regime's most prominent nativists love to make this claim, even as their intent is to end legal immigration, just as we did, more or less, during the 1920s.

And yet a more absurd proposition is difficult to imagine, given a government that encourages underground migration and suppresses official migration with every resource at its disposal. An immigrant is always in a tenuous situation—as our predecessors knew well, before we formalized whom we wanted and whom we didn't want—as he or she moves from temporary to permanent, denizen to resident, illegal to legal, or in the reverse direction, with ambiguity clouding the definition at any given time.

Before neoliberalism reshaped immigration in the 1990s, professional workers used to be in extended limbo, because their status, once they were sponsored by an employee, wasn't exactly clear. They were not supposed to be here, but they were, and already working for their sponsor, based on the probability that their labor certification would be approved. We never had a problem with "illegality" in the case of professionals, though we have cleared things up in their favor quite a bit since then.

On the other hand, what is your status if you applied as a refugee from, say, Central America twenty or thirty years ago? Your application was provisionally approved, but has fallen into limbo; a deportation order has not been issued, but your status has lapsed. We wanted you when there was a "Soviet-sponsored" Marxist insurgency we were fighting, but we don't care about you when we've decided to leave homegrown turmoil alone. Meanwhile, you've gone to school, had children, started a business, employ workers, and pay taxes. Your children are allowed to sponsor you when they come of age. Shortly before they are able to do so, are you legal or illegal? Do you become legal the day they apply for you, or do you have to wait until approval? In the years it might take immigration to decide your case, are you legal or illegal?[1]

---

[1] As of late 2017, the Trump administration has signaled its intention to cancel Temporary Protected Status (TPS) for hundreds of thousands of Haitians, Salvadorans, and Nicaraguans who have been in the country for many years, often long enough to have started families and businesses.
https://www.washingtonpost.com/world/national-security/trump-administration-to-end-provisional-residency-for-200000-

Many of us know of such ambiguous situations, which apply to all migrants, except those that corporate America has desired unreservedly over the last thirty years, since we brought immigration into line with neoliberal economic needs. Our federal immigration laws consist of layers upon layers of irrational, inconsistent, even bizarre and inexplicable exceptions, preferences, loopholes, punishments, waivers, mandates, and discretions that render the division between "legal" and "illegal" meaningless.

3. Immigration law is by nature exclusionary and racist.

We didn't always have a federal immigration bureaucracy. The idea began in the 1870s and 1880s, when we had finished building the railroads and accomplished enough developmental goals to feel that we could dispense with cheap imported labor. The presence of large numbers of Chinese and other Asians on the West Coast was leading to the same complaints about unfair job competition that we hear today, buttressed by the same inflammatory rhetoric. The racist Chinese Exclusion Act of 1882 was our first immigration law, setting the tone for our federal bureaucracy ever since then.

For Justice Stephen Johnson Field who ruled on the first important case upholding exclusion, *Chae Chan Ping v. United States* (1889),[1] the Chinese "remained strangers in the land," forever alien and unassimilable. We went from individual states setting the conditions for immigration to a federal bureaucracy founded on excluding a subpar race from tainting our racial stock.

From our foundation until our first immigration laws, our openness allowed us to successfully assimilate immigrants of diverse origins, all of whom had at first been looked upon suspiciously, such as the Germans and the Irish. Once we established a federal bureaucracy, it needed continuous rationales to sustain itself and to grow. From excluding the Chinese we moved to the Japanese, and

---

salvadorans/2018/01/08/badfde90-f481-11e7-beb6-c8d48830c54d_story.html?utm_term=.670664331dae.
[1] https://en.wikipedia.org/wiki/Chae_Chan_Ping_v._United_States.

then eastern and southern Europeans along with Jews, followed by subversives during the Cold War, and finally Muslims and Arabs as the latest target of exclusion.

Some of us may be under the illusion that we follow objective criteria to decide who comes in and who stays, observing standards that make moral, economic, or political sense. That has never been the case since the beginning of federal immigration policy.

The targets vary, but the logic remains the same. At the beginning of the twentieth century, progressives, trade unionists, eugenicists, and respectable politicians of all stripes were angered by large numbers of "inferior," disease-carrying, non-English speaking southern and eastern Europeans, so we shut them out with the 1924 national origins quota system, and decided instead to unofficially bring in large numbers of Mexicans.

We preferred Mexican immigrants persisting in limbo to European immigrants we would have to accommodate as citizens. We just had to make sure to periodically evict them from territorial assertion, as we did during the Great Depression, and as we did when we followed up the Bracero Program (importing guest workers)[1] with Operation Wetback (mass deportation),[2] a pattern that repeats to this day. We may say that we had an unofficial Bracero Program since the beginning of NAFTA until today, but we now want to expel the labor force.

Our history of exclusion is inherent in the nature of the bureaucracy and in all the laws that have been passed to empower it. During World War II we decided not to admit Jews seeking refuge from the European inferno. The logic of Asian exclusion easily led to the internment of Japanese Americans by our most progressive president.[3] Today we willfully exclude some of the best and brightest amongst us, if they happen to be Latino or Muslim or Arab. Exclusion affects whole classes of people and causes great national damage each time.

---

[1] http://braceroarchive.org/about.

[2] https://www.npr.org/sections/thetwo-way/2015/11/11/455613993/it-came-up-in-the-debate-here-are-3-things-to-know-about-operation-wetback.

[3] https://www.archives.gov/education/lessons/japanese-relocation.

4. The contemporary havoc goes back to the 1996 law.

But the repugnant national origins quota system, the internment of a whole race of people and the persecution of individuals because of political beliefs are all things well in the past, right? We don't do these things anymore, do we? After all, what was the great liberalization of the 1960s all about, if not to end such practices?

In reality, some of the most barbaric practices we as a nation have followed in terms of removal, slavery, and exclusion have come back in full force due to a reconceptualization of immigration under the 1996 law called IIRIRA (the Illegal Immigration Reform and Immigrant Responsibility Act). The key word here is "responsibility," used in a twisted neoliberal manner, placing burdens that are not so much responsibilities as refusals of humanity.

Though Trump's so-called "travel ban"[1] has been getting much of the attention lately, the infinitely greater area of concern is his targeting of every immigrant as potentially a "criminal alien" subject to "expedited removal." The authority Trump needs to put his genocidal plan into action was gifted to him under the 1996 law. It vastly expanded the definition of crimes and included everything from shoplifting to child neglect as "aggravated felonies" leading to deportation without appeal. "Expedited removal" means that the traditional safeguards offered to those under deportation proceedings are gone, and prosecutorial discretion is limited to the point of nonexistence.

The distinction between legal and illegal is intentionally blurred in such laws. "Aggravated felonies" retroactively subject not just undocumented people but legal permanent residents to deportation. Countless permanent residents have fallen under the net of this repressive law, one of the worst in our nation's history. Years or decades ago someone may have copped a guilty plea to a misdemeanor to get a lighter sentence, as is common in our criminal justice system. An encounter with the police, bringing the earlier "crime" to light, may abruptly destroy that person's life.

---

[1] https://en.wikipedia.org/wiki/Executive_Order_13769.

The 1996 law severely curtails the chances of refugees for having a fair hearing, while asylum seekers are presumed guilty when making a claim and put in mandatory detention that can last for years. Families who have experienced torture in countries that we have often had a hand in destabilizing are then placed in detention amongst hardened criminals, and made to wait for years before knowing their fate.

The 1996 law was part of the same movement toward "personal responsibility"—which is an euphemism for blaming victims for social crimes against them and then punishing them to boot—that also resulted in ending welfare, and expanding the reach of anti-terrorism in a law that became a precursor to the Patriot Act. These three laws—on immigration, welfare, and terrorism—overlap, for instance in curtailing judicial review, or ending public assistance for legal immigrants.

5. Neoliberalism is the main cause of the present "illegality."

So-called illegality is purely a self-created bureaucratic problem, which it is convenient for the neoliberal state to address as a criminal matter. It comes in handy because it keeps the lid on demands for democracy across racial lines, and it maintains a permanent underclass without rights, acting as a counterweight against universal fairness in the workplace.

The modern problem of illegality began in 1994, when NAFTA was passed. NAFTA offered a set of advantages to American big business and agriculture, creating tremendous pressure on Mexican small industry and farms and leading to the displacement of millions of workers, many of whom headed north. NAFTA freed capital movement at the same time as it restricted labor movement. So on the one hand, we created dire pressure for migration northward—to call it "push and pull" seems disingenuous, as though referring to inexorable laws of economics—at the same time as we cut off pathways to legal migration.

Before the 1990s, we always had a pattern of circular migration from Mexico. Migrants came and went; they didn't necessarily want to stay for good. Almost thirty million Mexicans entered the country between the start of the Bracero Program and the 1986 immigration law, but most of them went back. But the neoliberal regime made the price of mobility prohibitive. Border controls became so repressive, and the price of reentry so high, that most decided to put down roots. The children of these migrants have become the Dreamers[1] we now so proudly claim are the immigrants worthiest of our compassion.

When we wanted cheap agricultural labor we willfully let in large numbers of immigrants whom we did not want to assimilate. And now that the latest phase of globalization has run its course, the Trump regime wants to repatriate these people, long resident in our country, back "home." We can always crack the wall open a bit when later we need a new burst of cheap labor.

Under neoliberalism, we shuffle off unwanted labor to our private detention system, which daily commits horrors on a scale worthy of some of history's worst nightmares. Our policy preference is to put immigrants in detention for long periods of time before expelling them, so that they become revenue-earners for private prisons.[2] Under Trump we are about to witness a massive resurgence of the private prison industry, which lobbies for criminalization of immigrants.[3]

6. Comprehensive Immigration Reform (CIR) is always a boondoggle.

In every version it appears, CIR, a favorite prescription of both major political parties, is nothing but a Trojan horse to sneak in and formalize existing inhuman practices. Each CIR bill has been increasingly regressive, starting with the one that actually passed, Ronald Reagan's 1986 IRCA (Immigration Reform and Control Act).

---

[1] https://www.theguardian.com/us-news/2017/sep/04/donald-trump-what-is-daca-dreamers.

[2] http://thehill.com/blogs/congress-blog/homeland-security/365091-trumps-other-wall-private-immigration-jails-planned.

[3] https://www.motherjones.com/crime-justice/2017/12/private-prison-companies-are-about-to-cash-in-on-trumps-deportation-regime/.

Every CIR attempts three things: 1. It further criminalizes and delegalizes growing categories of people, reducing pathways to citizenship, while offering some sort of legal status to those few who qualify within increasingly narrow boundaries; 2. It seeks to convert immigrants into guest workers to the extent possible, implementing a regime that strays from linear outcomes; and 3. As a bargaining chip to sway restrictionists, who may have problems even with limited forms of legal status, it implements new policing measures to harden the already militarized border.

CIR is no solution. The 2006, 2007, and 2013 bills were each more draconian than their predecessors. The last one, under Obama, was much harsher than the ones Bush wanted. Militarization, which already stands at mind-boggling levels, with more than twenty thousand border patrol agents, would have gone up drastically in each CIR bill. To the extent that a wall can exist, it already does.[1] Each time a CIR bill is proposed, its legalization provisions don't become reality, but its militaristic provisions come true by other means.

Ever since the 1970s—with the arrival of Southeast Asian and Caribbean refugees, and the growing visibility of Asians in our population—sharply restrictionist moves have been packaged as CIR. Environmentalist John Tanton has been at the fount of most recent anti-immigrant advocacy.[2] His organization FAIR (Federation for American Immigration Reform),[3] along with associated organizations such as CIS (Center for Immigration Studies)[4] and NumbersUSA,[5] seeks to end legal immigration.[6] CIR bills have moved this goal closer

---

[1] http://theweek.com/captured/683638/border-wall-that-already-exists.

[2] http://www.detroitnews.com/story/news/michigan/2017/03/15/mich-man-led-immigration-fight-nearly-forgotten/99193990/.

[3] http://www.nytimes.com/2011/04/17/us/17immig.html?pagewanted=all&mtrref=www.google.com&gwh=A60FCB03A1CD65B6D293E2721E4B5649&gwt=pay.

[4] https://www.splcenter.org/hatewatch/2016/11/07/anti-immigrant-center-immigration-studies-continues-promote-white-nationalists.

[5] https://www.mediamatters.org/blog/2013/02/21/us-news-ignores-racist-ties-and-history-of-nati/192755.

[6] The Trump administration, as expected, is using temporary reprieve for Dreamers, following Trump's own suspension of the DACA program, as leverage in a grand strategy to end, or severely curtail, legal immigration once and for all. The

and closer in sight, until Trump can almost smell victory. FAIR and its affiliated organizations are consulted by the press on every policy move, and given equal footing with the vast array of pro-immigrant groups.

7. The "Dreamers" have been a destructive wedge issue.

This relates to my point about some immigrants offered ambiguous legalization, rather than universal access to citizenship offered to everyone under predictable conditions. The "Dreamers" are the splinter group artfully deployed to silence the demand for rights for all other immigrants.[1]

The concept of the Dreamers arose in the early 2000s (Democrat Dick Durbin was an early proponent), once the 1996 legislation had had time to work its way through the system, creating further avenues for "illegality." Instead of welcoming the *immigrant*, as we had done through all our history, we would welcome only the *Dreamer*. Anyone not certifiably a Dreamer would not belong.

What exactly is a Dreamer? A Dreamer is the postmodern version of a slave, embodying the idea of the pliant immigrant we seem most comfortable with. The Dreamer is *brought here against his will* (evoking the rhetoric of slavery), yet harbors no resentment toward the white majority who have enslaved his people. The Dreamer is not expected to mind that his parents may not be recognized as persons, even if present in the community for decades. The Dreamer willingly pays for college out of pocket, putting up with all the obstacles strewn by anti-

---

principles FAIR, CIS, and NumbersUSA have always desired, reorienting immigration toward sharply reduced numbers of only northern and western European immigrants, are reflected in new Trump administration proposals: https://www.vox.com/policy-and-politics/2018/1/25/16929600/trump-immigration-bill.

[1] The entire immigration discourse has shrunk to the rights of the Dreamers, to the exclusion of the other ten million undocumented immigrants, or refugees and asylum seekers, not to mention the vast pool of potential future immigrants who would be affected in a move to end future immigration, particularly in the form of family unification, all in order to secure some provisional status for the Dreamers.

immigrant states, particularly in the south and southwest. The Dreamer is unashamedly invested in the capitalist dream that he will have to purchase, as a consumer not a citizen. The Dreamer is expected to be grateful for grudging symbols of identity, a temporary work permit or a driver's license. The Dreamer begs to be granted the least token of recognition in return for partaking in our collective dream.

What about the elderly and disabled, the creative and artistic, the bohemian and nonconformist, all those not employed in the professions neoliberalism elevates? What about the parents of Dreamers? What about those who have committed any transgressions? They don't count as Dreamers, they are "criminal aliens."

The Dreamer is seen as accepting exclusion as a principle in return for being made a provisional part of our nationhood. No doubt Trump will use the Dreamers to split the rest from this small slice, to whom he might grant minimum concessions on the road to ending legal immigration. The Dreamers would be expected to go along, because all CIR bills, Obama's included, have separated the "good" from the "bad."

8. Immigrant rights are human rights.

There is a debate whether constitutional rights extend to all "persons" present in the United States, or only to citizens. The Constitution clearly says that rights belong to persons, not just citizens. Today the rights of non-citizens are being abridged as perhaps never before, and the need is paramount for the defense of immigrants having all constitutional rights.

Are freedom of speech and association, due process, and equal rights limited to citizens? Such would not seem to be the case if we look at much of our judicial history. There is plenty of judicial precedent for those who want to construct a vision for constitutional rights applying to all persons.

When the Chinese Exclusion Act set up the federal bureaucracy, states such as California and Arizona started passing legislation discriminating against immigrants. The courts held at the time that equal protection applied to persons, not just citizens, for example in striking down laws that discriminated against Chinese owners of laundries in California. And in *Truaux v. Raich*,[1] the Supreme Court held in 1915 that Arizona could not restrict the employment of immigrants.

The important recent landmark case is *Plyler v. Doe* (1982),[2] where the Supreme Court held that Texas was obligated to provide access to K-12 education to all persons, regardless of status. In succeeding years, the precedent set by *Plyler*, when it comes to immigrants' right to public services necessary for a fulfilling life, has not been consistently applied. Also, if K-12 access is vital, then isn't the same true of higher education?

We tend to assume that persons present on our soil have access to constitutional rights, at the very least the right to due process and habeas corpus (which, by the way, was stripped from immigrants in the 2005 REAL ID Act).[3] In reality, we have intentionally created a vast population of essentially stateless or displaced persons, refusing to extend constitutional rights to them, regardless of the letter and spirit of our founding documents.

Once we go down that path and create two regimes of law, one for citizens and one for everyone else, then it is inevitable that the regime created for immigrants will start affecting citizens as well, and constitutional rights will become restricted for all, as indeed has been the case in the last few decades. We cannot pretend anymore that what happens to "them," as immigrants, does not affect "us," as citizens. In every area of law, from the rights of consumers against corporations to the rights of citizens against the police, we have seen a drastic diminishment. Much of that has to do with our callousness toward immigrants.

---

[1] https://www.law.cornell.edu/supremecourt/text/239/33.

[2] https://www.law.cornell.edu/supremecourt/text/457/202.

[3] https://www.wsws.org/en/articles/2005/05/id-m26.html.

9. The president has almost unlimited powers.

To the extent that Trump will be able to get his ban against Muslim immigration approved by the courts (and we seem to be headed toward extension to more Muslim countries),[1] it will be because of the plenary power doctrine.

The courts, ever since the federal immigration bureaucracy came into being, have ceded vast powers to the executive to set the guidelines for immigration. Trump will make full use of this authority, some of it latent, some of it used by other presidents.

Chae Chan Ping (1889), mentioned above, was the first case, soon after the Chinese Exclusion Act, where the plenary power doctrine became inscribed, justifying the government's power to exclude. After World War II, several landmark cases decided amidst cold war paranoia—*Knauff v. Shaughnessy* (1950),[2] *Harisiades v. Shaughnessy* (1952),[3] and *Shaughnessy v. Mezei* (1953)[4]—reaffirmed plenary power. Immigrants trying to return to the country were stopped or detained, based on alleged subversive views. Granting such unlimited powers is only asking for trouble when an unscrupulous administration comes along to take undue advantage.

Trump will test the limits of the plenary power doctrine with a range of executive orders and legislative initiatives.[5] The only check on his power to do with immigrants as he wishes is for the courts to return firmly to precedents where limits on plenary power have been acknowledged. And for the courts to take a stand against the existence of this power in the first place.

---

[1] https://www.npr.org/2017/09/24/553353302/trump-administration-revises-travel-ban-expands-beyond-muslim-majority-countries.

[2] https://supreme.justia.com/cases/federal/us/338/537/case.html.

[3] https://supreme.justia.com/cases/federal/us/342/580/case.html.

[4] https://supreme.justia.com/cases/federal/us/345/206/case.html.

[5] http://www.scotusblog.com/2017/07/symposium-end-plenary-power/.

10. Open borders are the only way to go.

We are in a situation of chaos, breeding technical illegality, because federal regulations have become too complex. CIR of any type would make these laws even more cumbersome, by drastically curtailing family unification (our quotas, even after the 1965 liberalization, have always been vastly insufficient to the needs) and thus inviting more illegality. I don't want to rest my case for open borders on the economic justification, but studies in the 1980s noted that world economic output would double if there were open borders everywhere, and studies in the 2000s showed even greater gains for the world economy.

Americans often compare the nation to a house, arguing that immigrants who enter without inspection or overstay their visas are like robbers whom we have every right to detain and expel. But a country, or even a state or a city or a neighborhood, is not a house (just as it is simplistic to compare a country's budget to a household's). The nation is dynamic, and includes all of us. The nation is an abstraction only as good as the operation of freedom within it. The same is even truer of the world. And if the world cannot be put inside a border, then a country trying to do the same is foolish.

A wall is a fantasy, not a reality, that makes us economically and politically weaker. None of the moral grounds for exclusion make any sense, despite our knee-jerk resort to national sovereignty. Imagine if America had kept admitting Asians throughout the nineteenth and twentieth centuries, instead of only allowing them after 1965. Imagine if we had continued allowing southern and eastern Europeans after 1925. Would we have been a more progressive country, less likely to have succumbed to the burdens of an empire, with a more global outlook in the crucial mid-century years?

Today immigrants are treated as criminals for their violations, with deportation as the ultimate life-altering penalty, and yet immigrants are not provided the rights due to a criminal defendant. Immigration is and always has been a civil matter; it is not a crime to be present without authorization. We have in essence two sets of laws, one for immigrants, who do not have the rights of defendants when charged with "crimes," and one for everyone else. The only solution to this anomaly is to cease treating immigration violations as crimes, and for there to be a complete end to detention for immigration. If an immigrant commits a crime, he or she should be prosecuted under normal laws, as a criminal defendant, not as a "criminal alien."

Ultimately, the only solution is to reduce the complexities, to end the web of regulations and exceptions—which, just as in corporate law, favor the powerful at the expense of the weak—and finally to do away with immigration laws altogether.

Immigration should become a purely voluntary affair, no different than filing taxes. We trust citizens to do that, reporting millions of dollars in income, so why can't we trust people to report their status and to file for changes based on equities they have built in our community? As soon as a person steps on our soil, he should have full constitutional rights, so that he is not subject to exploitation. Why can't we visualize immigration without government regulation? We certainly did very well with that regime until the federal bureaucracy emerged in the 1880s, and with revived global understanding we can do so again.

Some concluding thoughts.

Trump is taking advantage, for white nationalist purposes, of a legacy of tragically unfair rules that have defined our immigration system ever since it's existed. We are now bearing the full fruits of a system that was begging to end in catastrophe.

In the first six months of 2011, more than forty-six thousand immigrants with at least one U.S. citizen child were deported by the Obama administration. In the ten years after passage of the 1996 law, more than twelve million people were forced to agree to voluntary departure! Though ICE under Trump is dramatically apprehending immigrants in public venues—a theater of cruelty meant to terrorize everyone—and causing great consternation, this exact process of splitting up families has been going on for two vicious decades, in numbers that classify as one of the world's major human rights calamities.

Countless numbers of immigrants, even legal permanent residents, have been hauled away from their families, their communities, everything they know and love, based on some minor misdemeanor they may have committed decades ago, which has suddenly been reclassified as an "aggravated felony," and is cause for their deportation to places they have no memory of. Such immigrants do not have the right to be heard by a judge except in a perfunctory manner, with little room for clemency based on individual circumstances.

We do not call them concentration camps, but at any given time we have around thirty-four thousand immigrants in mandatory detention,[1] serving time in prisons far from home, awaiting to be deported before serving out their mandatory punishment. Is this any different than the prison regimes of the most brutal governments we have protested in the past?

Migration is a human right. A person anywhere in the world has the right to migrate, just as there is a right to free speech or association. In fact, most other rights follow from the right to migrate. If governments are allowed to lock up people behind walls, then it's only a matter of time before other rights will dissipate too. If we do not recognize migration as an inviolable human right, and if we do not give up the idea of the wall, we are bound to lose human rights for all of us.

American citizenship, by having become associated with the hypernationalist project, will at first look enviable and untouchable, but ultimately will be so cheapened as to be worth nothing. For the courts, as they face the Trump assault, the challenge is clear: Do away with the plenary power doctrine, and extend full constitutional rights to immigrants. Rights should depend on personhood, not citizenship, as some of our best legal minds have recognized throughout our history.

One thing that would strongly push the country in the opposite direction than the one Trump intends is for individual states, particularly progressive states in the west or northeast, to pass laws as favorable to immigrants as the ones in Arizona, Georgia, and Alabama have been unfavorable. What if, say, California were to pass legislation extending full human rights to all persons present in the

---

[1] https://www.immigrantjustice.org/eliminate-detention-bed-quota.

state? That would set up a historic confrontation, bringing out all the anomalies in our inhuman immigration regime for due public consideration.[1] "Sanctuary" would become a constructive, constitutional, universal concept, not a purely reactive one against police powers.

And one final note. Every time we say that we should let immigrants stay because they do the dirtiest work the natives aren't willing to do, we should remember that we do not justify our own ancestors' arrival with that logic. We deserve to be here because we have a human right to do so, just as we accepted this in the centuries preceding racist federal bureaucracies. We are here because we are humans, not because of our utility toward someone else's comfort.

---

[1] Initiatives like this are a small start: http://www.newsweek.com/immigrants-are-getting-right-vote-cities-across-america-664467.

Immigration Roundtable:
Three Top Immigration Scholars Address the Most Pressing Immigration Controversies

Big changes are afoot on immigration policy, as the right continues to deploy its familiar talking points, feeding into the Trump punitive juggernaut. Unfortunately, the current public discourse—whether it's the Muslim ban or the expulsion of so-called "criminal aliens"—remains mostly free of historical, legal, and philosophical nuance. We are lurching from one dramatic executive order to another without much sense of how we got here and what are the realistic remedies we can pursue. If we are going to move forward on immigration, we need to immerse ourselves in the concrete historical and constitutional dilemmas that have led to the current crisis.

Here to add nuance to the immigration debate are three of the nation's foremost experts on immigration, criminal justice, and constitutional law, taking on not only what we already know about Trump's travel ban and deportation policy but also expected future initiatives from this administration. These scholars address the thorniest issues in immigration, the ones at the root of our present crisis, with all the ballast we need to oppose simplistic talking points: Should immigrants, regardless of status, have constitutional rights? How solid in law and morality is Trump's reliance on the plenary power doctrine to implement far-reaching changes? Is Trump's deportation policy an anomaly, or does it have roots in recent bipartisan legislation? And what can the states, as a last resort, do to counter federal anti-immigration initiatives?

John S. W. Park is chair and professor of Asian American Studies at the University of California at Santa Barbara. He is a specialist in race theory, immigration law and policy, and Anglo-American legal and political theory. His influential books include *Elusive Citizenship: Immigration, Asian Americans, and the Paradox of Civil Rights*, *Probationary Americans: Contemporary Immigration Policies and the Shaping of Asian American Communities*, with Edward J. W. Park, and *Illegal Migrations and the Huckleberry Finn Problem*.

Kevin R. Johnson is Mabie-Apallas Professor of Public Interest Law, Professor of Chicana/o Studies, and Dean at the University of California at Davis School of Law. His widely referenced books include *How Did You Get to Be Mexican? A White/Brown Man's Search for Identity* and *Immigration Law and the U.S.-Mexico Border*. He is president of the board of directors of Legal Services of Northern California and has served on the board of the Mexican American Legal Defense and Education Fund (MALDEF). He blogs at ImmigrationProf and SCOTUSblog.

David Brotherton is professor of sociology at the John Jay College of Criminal Justice at the City University of New York (CUNY). His recent books include *Keeping Out The Other: A Critical Introduction to Immigration Control*, edited with Philip Kretsedemas, and *The Almighty Latin King and Queen Nation: Street Politics and the Transformation of a New York City Gang*, with Luis Barrios. His current research projects include a performance-based sociological study of immigration removal hearings in New York City.

The constitutional rights of immigrants.

Do constitutional rights depend on citizenship or personhood? In other words, should immigrants, regardless of status, have full constitutional rights? Why, or why not? Should such rights commence as soon as a person steps foot on U.S. soil? If you wish to grant immigrants some but not all constitutional rights, which ones are you excluding and why?

John S.W. Park

Until the Fourteenth Amendment, the United States Supreme Court and other federal institutions did not behave as though the constitution should apply to non-citizens. For example, President John Adams supported the Alien and Sedition Acts[1] in 1798, a rule that, among other things, gave the President the authority to deport foreigners whom he considered hostile to the United States, and then lengthened the number of years of residency required for new immigrants to petition for American citizenship, from five years to fourteen. Adams did not think that new immigrants (especially French radicals fresh from their own bloody Revolution) should be able to vote after just five years here, and he felt that all "radicals" should be deported. He was appalled that Thomas Jefferson, his political rival, had praised the French Revolution, and Adams thought the rules in 1798 necessary to protect the republic from foreigners.

Not two decades later, President Andrew Jackson insisted that Native Americans were not American citizens, and thus also not eligible for constitutional protections. He and his supporters noted that the phrase, "Indians not taxed," appeared in the original constitution, in that portion where they were expressly excluded from congressional representation. Moreover, Congress had passed the Naturalization Act of 1790, less than two years after the constitution's ratification, and under the Act of 1790, only "free white persons" could pass into American citizenship. "Indians not taxed" and persons of African ancestry, including slaves, were not "white" or "free" and so, in the words of Justice Taney in *Dred Scott* (1857),[2] persons of African ancestry also had "no rights which the white man [was] bound to respect." Andrew Jackson had appointed Roger Taney to the United States Supreme Court, and both men interpreted the constitution to exclude Native Americans and persons of African ancestry from American citizens.

After the Civil War, the framers of the Thirteenth, Fourteenth, and Fifteenth Amendments attempted to resolve these problems in

---

[1] http://www.ushistory.org/us/19e.asp.

[2] https://en.wikipedia.org/wiki/Dred_Scott_v._Sandford.

favor of more expansive definitions for constitutional rights. The Thirteenth abolished slavery, and the Fifteenth guaranteed the right to vote, but the Fourteenth amendment[1] said that anyone born on American territory should be regarded as an American citizen. In addition, the radical Republicans insisted that personhood, not citizenship, should be enough to trigger constitutional protections: "Nor shall any state deprive any *person* of life, liberty, or property, without due process of law…nor deny to any *person* within its jurisdiction the equal protection of the laws."

Chinese immigrants in California would force the federal courts to clarify the meaning and scope of these passages: In *Yick Wo* (1886),[2] for example, the United States Supreme Court struck down San Francisco rules that were meant to harass Chinese residents of that city, under the theory that they were "persons" within the protections of the Fourteenth Amendment. However, just three years later (and over the next fifty years), this same Court said the United States could exclude all immigrants, including former Chinese migrants, if Congress chose to do so. Justice Stephen Field said that the Fourteenth Amendment circumscribed the "states," not so much the federal government, and with respect to foreigners, the United States should have broad powers to exclude persons it didn't want. In *Wong Kim Ark* (1898),[3] the Court said that Chinese persons born in the United States were American citizens not subject to exclusion, but this proved a rare victory. In most other cases, the Court upheld the right of the United States to exclude prospective immigrants, and it gave the President broad discretion to determine how best to do that, under the idea that newcomers were persons, but not yet members of the United States. In cases where the federal government had behaved perhaps too severely toward newcomers, the Court offered immigrants *procedural* protections designed to curb zealous immigration enforcement. People who claimed citizenship, for example, should have the right to present evidence of their citizenship before being summarily deported.

---

[1] https://www.law.cornell.edu/constitution/amendmentxiv.
[2] https://en.wikipedia.org/wiki/Yick_Wo_v._Hopkins.
[3] https://www.law.cornell.edu/supremecourt/text/169/649.

Over the years, the federal courts have said that persons who've resided in the United States, and even persons who've had longer term relationships with the American government, should have similar procedural rights under the constitution, and in some rough proportion to the length of their stay or their relationship. This is why deporting a long-time resident, even someone without legal immigration status, tends to be more complicated than deporting someone who just arrived. This is also why, when the United States holds someone in Guantánamo Bay for a longer (indefinite?) period of time, the federal courts have demanded some procedural protections for these inmates, even though they're not citizens and they're not *in* the United States, as in *Hamdan* (2006).[1]

Does the constitution protect citizens or all persons? The fundamental problem might rest in a basic philosophical disagreement about the constitution itself. Is the constitution a kind of contract that primarily benefits and binds American citizens to one another? Or is it a broader statement of principles—perhaps reflecting commitments to fairness and justice and other important values—that are distinctive of a classical Enlightenment moment? We still debate these questions. The late Justice Scalia was a strong proponent of the former view, while many leading scholars and jurists—Justice Ginsburg, or Bruce Ackerman of Yale or Mark Tushnet of Harvard—have argued the other side.

Imagine a case where our officials go to a foreign country and suppress its press and media organs, maybe assassinate a journalist or two—does this kind of behavior raise a "constitutional" problem? Scalia might say that such things are illegal in those countries, but it's not an American *constitutional* violation because it took place abroad, where the constitution isn't binding, and to victims who did not have American constitutional rights. Progressive scholars might say, however, that the constitution represents collective commitments to certain basic values—protections for a free and vibrant press, and free speech rights in general—and that Americans violate those principles when they suppress those rights wherever they are, even when the victims are not fellow Americans. Because of these fundamentally

---

[1] https://en.wikipedia.org/wiki/Hamdan_v._Rumsfeld.

different perspectives, people in constitutional debates often speak past each other, one side thinking that the status of the victim, the status of the perpetrator, and the location of the purported violation are all important, while the other side considers these things not as relevant.

Consider how the constitution might be similar to a set of "house rules." In my house, for example, we take our shoes off, we don't believe children should talk back to their parents, and we observe excellent table manners. If my kid goes to someone else's house, however, and then traipses around with her shoes on, shoves her face with food, and curses like a sailor, what to do? Should I punish her when she gets home, and is it my responsibility that she not behave like a brat in *anyone's* house? Is she a representative of my family, constrained by the expectations of her parents wherever she goes?

And what can I reasonably expect of other children who come over to my house? Can I say, for example, "Take your shoes off (you little white barbarian)," and then kick out the ones who don't obey? Do I have the right not to invite ill-mannered, dangerous children, say, pyromaniac kids or kids with full-blown influenza?

What if my wife and I adopt a child, and what if the kid lives with us for several years, utterly mindful of our rules—would we be heartless to chuck her out for a minor infraction? What if we didn't legally adopt the kid, but she's lived with us nonetheless, and we didn't remove her either because our house is so gigantic and we've noticed that she does the dishes and takes out the trash, year after year. Are we wrong if, one day, we tell her to leave, either because she didn't observe the no-shoe policy or we're just tired of her?

Kevin R. Johnson

a) Due Process rights of non-citizens physically present in the United States.

The protections of the U.S. Constitution extend to all persons, including all immigrants, physically present in the United States. The Fifth and Fourth Amendments prevent both federal and state governments from depriving any *person* of "life, liberty, or property without due process of law." "Liberty" includes, but is not limited to, freedom from detention and freedom from removal from the United States.

The U.S. Supreme Court has held that, before they can be removed from the United States, non-citizens—no matter their immigration status (*i.e.*, *undocumented immigrants have due process rights*)—are entitled to a hearing that complies with Due Process. Consider *Yamataya v. Fisher*[1] (The Japanese Immigrant Case), 189 U.S. 86 (1903). Because of the weighty interests of the non-citizen at stake, *Fong Haw Tan v. Phelan*,[2] 333 U.S. 6, 10 (1948) ("Deportation is a drastic measure and at times the equivalent of banishment or exile."); *Bridges v. Wixon*,[3] 326 U.S. 135, 147 (1945) (emphasizing that "deportation may result in the loss *'of all that makes life worth living'*") (citation omitted) (emphasis added), a removal hearing is constitutionally required.

Today, an immigration court, an administrative tribunal housed in the U.S. Department of Justice, holds a hearing in which the U.S. government seeks to remove a non-citizen from the United States. Removal hearings allow the government and the non-citizen to present witnesses, and to submit documentary evidence. The immigration court's decision is reviewed by an administrative Board of Immigration Appeals (BIA). The BIA ruling can be appealed to a U.S. court of appeals. The Supreme Court has consistently held that, even when Congress appears to have eliminated judicial review of a removal order, the Constitution requires *some* kind of judicial review: *INS v. St. Cyr*,[4] 533 U.S. 289 (2001) (holding that, despite congressional restrictions on judicial review in 1996, removal orders must be reviewed by a federal district court through a writ of habeas corpus).

The precise Due Process rights of a non-citizen may vary by type of immigration status and length of time in the United States. In *Landon v. Plasencia*,[5] 459 U.S. 21 (1982), the Supreme Court

---

[1] https://en.wikipedia.org/wiki/Yamataya_v._Fisher.

[2] https://supreme.justia.com/cases/federal/us/333/6/.

[3] https://supreme.justia.com/cases/federal/us/326/135/.

[4] https://supreme.justia.com/cases/federal/us/533/289/.

[5] https://supreme.justia.com/cases/federal/us/459/21/.

addressed the constitutionality of the denial of entry into the United States of a long-term lawful permanent resident, Maria Plasencia, who had left the country for a weekend in Mexico. The Court acknowledged that "once an alien gains admission to our country and begins to develop the ties that go with permanent residence, his constitutional status changes accordingly. Our cases have frequently suggested that a continuously present resident alien is entitled to a fair hearing when threatened with deportation." The Court added that, in the case before it, "Plasencia was absent from the country only a few days, and *the United States has conceded that she has a right to due process.*" (emphasis added).

The Supreme Court directed that the *Mathews v. Eldridge*,[1] 425 U.S. 319 (1976) balancing test be used to determine the specific procedures that Due Process required in Plasencia's case: "The courts must consider the interest at stake for the individual, the risk of an erroneous deprivation of the interest through the procedures used as well as the probable value of additional or different procedural safeguards, and the interest of the government in using the current procedures rather than additional or different procedures."

The courts have read *Landon v. Plasencia* as requiring the application of the balancing test to determine whether immigration procedures are consistent with Due Process: *Zadvydas v. Davis*,[2] 533 U.S. 678, 694 (2002).

In sketching how the interests might be balanced in the case before it, the Court noted that Maria Plasencia, a lawful permanent resident, had a "weighty" interest at stake and "[stood] to lose the right 'to stay and live and work in this land of freedom,' with the possible loss of the right to rejoin her immediate family, a right that ranks high among the interests of the individual." (citation omitted). The Court also acknowledged the government's "weighty" interest in the efficient administration of the immigration laws. The Court instructed the lower court on remand to determine "whether the procedures

---

[1] https://www.casebriefs.com/blog/law/administrative-law/administrative-law-keyed-to-lawson/constitutional-constraints-on-agency-procedure/mathews-v-eldridge/.

[2] https://www.law.cornell.edu/supct/html/99-7791.ZS.html.

[applied to Plasencia] meet the *essential standard of fairness under the Due Process Clause.*" (emphasis added) (citation omitted).

b) Non-citizens' right to counsel.

Unlike the defendant in a criminal case, a non-citizen in removal proceedings is not guaranteed counsel by the U.S. Constitution. However, the Immigration and Nationality Act § 292, 8 U.S.C. § 1362 provides that "[i]n any removal proceedings before an immigration judge and in any appeal…, the person concerned shall have the privilege of being represented (*at no expense to the Government*) by such counsel, authorized to practice in such proceedings, as he shall choose." (emphasis added). Counsel is essential because of the complexity of the immigration laws: *Castro-O'Ryan v. INS*,[1] 847 F.2d 1307, 1312 (9th Cir. 1988) ("With only a small degree of hyperbole, the immigration laws have been termed 'second only to the Internal Revenue Code in complexity.'" (citation omitted); *Lok v. INS*,[2] 548 F.2d 37, 38 (2d Cir. 1977) (stating that U.S. immigration laws resemble "King Mino's labyrinth in ancient Crete"). Not surprisingly, non-citizens represented by counsel in removal proceedings are much more likely to prevail than those who are unrepresented: Ingrid V. Eagly & Steven Shafer, *A National Study of Access to Counsel in Immigration Court*, 164 U. PA. L. REV. 1 (2015).

Strong arguments have been made that Due Process requires that non-citizens be guaranteed counsel in removal proceedings: Kevin R. Johnson, *An Immigration* Gideon *for Lawful Permanent Residents,* 122 YALE L.J. 2394 (2013) (making this argument for lawful permanent residents in removal proceedings); Nimrod Pitsker, Comment, *Due Process for All: Applying* Eldridge *to Require Appointed Counsel for Asylum Seekers*, 95 CAL. L. REV. 169 (2007) (making similar arguments for asylum seekers). Some local jurisdictions with large immigrant populations, including Los Angeles and New York, have taken steps to increase access of immigrant residents to legal representation in

---

[1] https://openjurist.org/847/f2d/1307/castro-oryan-v-united-states-department-of-immigration-and-naturalization.

[2] https://openjurist.org/681/f2d/107/lok-v-immigration-and-naturalization-service.

removal proceedings. The California Legislature is considering measures that would provide funding to increase access to counsel for immigrants.

This discussion has focused on constitutional rights of persons, including non-citizens, physically present in the United States. Prospective immigrants outside the United States have more limited constitutional protections, as will be discussed below.

David Brotherton

My position on this is that anyone who steps on U.S. soil should be protected by the constitution. Of course, this does not include the right to vote or the right to run for elected office; these rights should remain those of citizens only. However, all other rights such as those that relate to the protections of individuals and groups provided under the U.S. legal code are applicable to anyone residing in the nation regardless of how long or short their stay. Some of the most important rights that should be enjoyed by all such as due process, protections against search and seizure, and the right to freedom of speech are critical democratic rights and should be understood not just as U.S. rights but as universal rights.

Since the U.S. is fond of declaring itself to be a paragon and exemplar of a functioning democracy it should set an example of ensuring that the rights that it holds so dear and which in its eyes make it such an exceptional nation-state should be available to all who pass through its borders. Of course, it would be wonderful if those constitutional rights of the U.S. could be extended in furtherance of establishing a more functioning and less contradictory participatory democracy, since it is clear that the extraordinary economic power of certain individuals and social classes has greatly thwarted the promise of the democratic project so many residents of the U.S., be they citizens or non-citizens, believe in and long for.

The plenary power doctrine.

Do you think that the plenary power doctrine, as it has been applied to federal immigration law for the last one hundred and twenty-five years, is too broad? In what ways would you restrict it, or would you do away with it altogether? What would be your basis in law for supporting abolition of the plenary power doctrine when it comes to immigration, if that is a position you support?

John S.W. Park

Public officials suggested the idea of "plenary power" prior to immigration law, and the idea originates in the relationship between the United States and Native American tribes. Native American tribes and Native American people were not citizens of the United States, even though they lived within the boundaries of the states. They were "domestic dependent nations," apart from the United States, and yet under the authority of the United States government as conquered people. For them, Congress and the President had "plenary power," and the federal courts had limited power to check these branches, even when the federal courts could acknowledge, as they did in *Cherokee Nation v. Georgia*[1] (1831), that Congress and President were not living up to their treaty obligations. Because Native Americans were not American citizens, and because the federal courts only protected the rights of American citizens under the constitution, injured Native Americans had to seek remedies from Congress and the President, not the federal courts, according to Chief Justice John Marshall. This line of thinking lasted well into the first half of the twentieth century.

In the immigration context, the federal courts were highly influenced by these precedents—in cases concerning immigrants and

---

[1] http://www.cherokee.org/About-The-Nation/History/Trail-of-Tears/Cherokee-Nation-v-State-of-Georgia.

non-citizens, they've held that the federal courts should not interfere with laws and policies established in Congress and by the President for non-citizens. Again, for people who believe that the Constitution was a kind of contract, designed primarily or exclusively for the benefit of American citizens, there is no moral or legal problem with this position. Congress should have the right to limit immigrants who seem harmful, to encourage those who might help the United States, and otherwise set the procedures and policies that govern entry, exclusion, and removal.

For those of us who feel that the Constitution represents statements of broad principles, however, the plenary powers doctrine has always been highly problematic. We note that the United States Supreme Court created this doctrine to justify doing nothing as Native Americans were driven off their ancestral lands. Then the Court used the same doctrine again when Congress moved to exclude Chinese immigrants in the late nineteenth century, as it also endorsed notions that the Chinese were a threat to white working-class people and that they were "unassimilable." Thus, the Court allowed Congress and the President to be stone-cold racist, in spite of the Fourteenth Amendment and the Civil War and lofty (re-)commitments to the equality of all people irrespective of race. It's very disturbing to think that these precedents are still "good law": the principle of Chinese Exclusion still survives, in the sense that if Congress and the President agree to exclude Muslims or Koreans or any group by race or nationality, many justices would likely not interfere.

Indeed, does the President now have the right to exclude people from Muslim nations, simply because they're Muslim? He will say that they are not citizens, that they are not yet in the United States, that precedents support this exercise of his executive power; others will say that such policies undermine commitments to religious liberty, in addition to other fundamental commitments implied within the equal protection and due process clauses. Again, these differences stem from inherent disagreements about the constitution, the scope of national sovereignty and then our commitment to broader principles reflected in the constitution.

Several scholars have argued that when individual nations pursue their own interests unchecked by international norms or standards (or even their own norms and standards), all kinds of bad things can happen. Especially when they've assessed the behavior of "criminal states," some scholars and officials have argued the need for international treaties and organizations that can hold government officials accountable when they violate basic human rights or behave in racist or genocidal ways. Samantha Power, the former U.S. Ambassador to the UN, has noted that state-sanctioned genocidal actions should *never* be lawful, and that robust international treaties and conventions are necessary to prevent these actions and to hold officials accountable. Such treaties would, by necessity, curb doctrines like the plenary powers doctrine, in cases where states may abuse or murder their own citizens or non-citizens.

Others say that such moves could tend toward "international tyranny" and "world government." Members of the Trump administration, including the President himself, have chafed against international organizations, including the UN, EU, NATO, WTO, the European Court of Human Rights, and so on. They've favored an "America First" that would allow all nation-states to pursue their own ends without international interference. The proponents of this "America First" idea say that in the postwar world, the United States has shouldered a disproportionate burden for the haphazard, imperfect international system that we have now—Trump has suggested scrapping the system, or making American allies pay more for American participation. He and many of his key advisors do not seem to think themselves, or this nation, as bound to international law or international organizations.

I and many other scholars believe that this approach could lead to disaster. To varying degrees, many of us believe that basic human equality within nation-states is a core value applicable not just in the U.S., but in all states. Conversely, state-sanctioned discriminations based on race, nationality, gender, political opinion, religion, and other similar characteristics are simply unjust—no state should harm or persecute anyone based on these grounds. Free speech and a free press, due process of law, political participation and representative government, rule of law, prohibitions against cruel and unusual punishment—these are all really good ideas that should bind all nations, too. I don't think it's a good idea to promote the right to bear arms (as an individual right), but I do think that many other provisions of the constitution embody excellent ideas that *already* curtail all government actors in the United States.

And thus I and many others would support international and national efforts to bring our own national sovereignty in line with those values—we should not admit or exclude immigrants on the basis of religion, gender, race, nationality, and so on. That is, faced with choices between plenary powers on the one hand and basic human rights norms on the other, I believe that Americans should always choose human rights norms, even if that means that we give up or circumscribe our own sovereignty. In this view, I am fine with handing over my own government officials if they've been accused of torture, or mass incarceration of their own citizens, or any other serious violation of international human rights norms. Yet of course, public officials who've entertained race-based exclusions and religious bars and torture aren't thrilled by that possibility.

These insights work forwards and backwards: I think the Nuremberg Trials after World War II were imperfect in many ways, but one of the deepest flaws may have lain in an unwillingness to subject American public officials to some harsh questions—did *they* commit crimes against humanity? Was it necessary to drop two atomic weapons? Should it ever be lawful to carpet bomb and incinerate whole cities? Was the incarceration of Japanese persons and Japanese Americans a state-level criminal act tinged with racism?

Kevin R. Johnson

In *The Chinese Exclusion Case*,[1] 130 U.S. 581 (1889), the Supreme Court upheld the Chinese Exclusion Act, which largely banned immigration from China to the United States. In so doing, the Court held that Congress had "plenary power" over immigration and its substantive immigration decisions were not subject to judicial review. The Chinese Exclusion Act was one of many racially discriminatory laws passed by Congress in the late 1800s, almost all of which were upheld by the courts.

---

[1] https://supreme.justia.com/cases/federal/us/130/581/case.html,

Over the last one hundred and twenty-five years, "cracks" have emerged in the plenary power doctrine. Namely, the Supreme Court at times has exercised minimal judicial review over immigration decisions: *Kerry v. Din*,[1] 135 S. Ct. 2128 (2015); *Kleindienst v. Mandel*,[2] 408 U.S. 753 (1972). In recent years, the Court has rarely invoked the plenary power doctrine and, indeed, on a number of occasions strived to avoid invoking it. The reason: The antiquated *Chinese Exclusion Case* is out of synch with the Supreme Court's modern constitutional jurisprudence. One would think that minimal rationality review of U.S. government action with respect to immigration would be more consistent with modern constitutional sensibilities than the immunity from judicial review bestowed by the plenary power doctrine.

Another factor militates in favor of judicial review of decisions of non-citizens seeking admission into the United States. In the average immigrant admission case, the rights of U.S. citizens and lawful permanent residents in the United States, such as family members and employers, are adversely affected by the denial of the admission of a person into the United States. In *Kerry v. Din*, 135 U.S. 2128 (2015), six Justices of the Supreme Court agreed that, when rights of a person in the United States are affected by a visa denial, as in cases such as *Kleindienst v.* Mandel (1972), judicial review of the decision is justified.

David Brotherton

The plenary power doctrine places the regulation of immigration and deportation firmly in the hands of the legislative and executive branches of the government. To some degree this makes sense since (as it is often argued) it is preferable for elected officials rather than appointed judges to hold sway over such important policy matters and practices relating to changes in national sovereignty and the application of human rights. Certainly, during the 1960s when the country was moving in a more liberal direction we can see how

---

[1] http://www.scotusblog.com/case-files/cases/kerry-v-din/.

[2] https://supreme.justia.com/cases/federal/us/408/753/case.html.

progressive changes to the immigration laws allowed a much more diverse population to enter the United States and end the privileging of Europe as the source of immigrant population flows, which had largely been the case hitherto.

However, obviously when Congress moves to the right or there is a surge in anti-immigrant feeling among the populace we can get the opposite as happened in 1996 with the racist and highly punitive Illegal Immigration Reform and Immigrant Responsibility Act (IIRIRA).[1] In this particular case we also see what happens when democratic decision-making is not in evidence and the much heralded checks and balance characteristic of U.S. legislative practice is not apparent. For example, as the renowned immigration lawyer Ira Kurzban wrote of the flawed process that led to the bill's passing:

Lamar Smith, who was the Chairman of the House Immigration Subcommittee at the time, rewrote the immigration laws by hiring lawyers from FAIR (Federation for Immigration Reform), an anti-immigration group. He knew he could not simply eliminate all waivers so he and his staff rewrote the waivers to make them far less useful to most people. The Republican members of Congress deferred to Smith and the Democrats were only provided the IIRIRA legislation less than seventy-two hours before there was a vote.

Kurzban went on to remind us that other than Smith, one of Congress's foremost deniers of climate change, almost no other legislator actually read the three hundred-plus page tome. Nonetheless, the acceptance of this critical piece of legislation has resulted in changes to the regulation of the country's borders, both internally and externally, with some of the most devastating effects on immigrant families ever recorded in the nation's history. I am referring here to the deportation of millions of U.S. residents, many of whom lived and worked here legally, and the collateral damage this has caused.

Consequently, when one sees this type of reactionary political shift in immigration policy due to the plenary power provision and how it has paved the way for the present insular, xenophobic and anti-

---

[1] https://en.wikipedia.org/wiki/Illegal_Immigration_Reform_and_Immigrant_Responsibility_Act_of_1996.

Muslim conception of border control, the current process cries out for modification and far greater democratic accountability. It should be remembered that Clinton called this particular legislation one of the worst he ever signed and assured the nation that it would be revised at a later stage. Alas, the only revisions made to the bill pushed the provisions therein further to the restrictionist and punitive right and nothing has been done since to alleviate its dire results.

The effects of the 1996 immigration law.

What are some of the most pernicious effects of the 1996 immigration legislation that you have experienced as a scholar or practitioner? Will the Trump administration be able to count on the "expedited removals" provision of the 1996 law, or even expand it, as it targets specific racial groups? How do you feel about retroactive punishment for minor transgressions, or any transgressions?

John S.W. Park

Indeed, Congress and President Bill Clinton passed a set of rules in 1996 that expanded the category of persons eligible for "removal," that limited common forms of relief for people facing removal and that made removal based on criminal convictions more "expedited." These rules said that judges could not consider relief in removal proceedings when the person facing removal had a criminal record. These rules governing "criminal aliens" were part of a broader set of legislative rules designed to reduce the "cost" of immigrants in general—new legal immigrants, for example, were ineligible for public assistance, and poorer American citizens and legal residents could no longer sponsor immigrants under family reunification provisions. By removing a much larger share of "criminal aliens," Congress thought that it could reduce financial burdens on the states and the federal government, in light of how they were spending money on law enforcement, criminal prosecution and incarceration for non-citizens. Many Americans still embrace the idea that non-citizens who misbehave must go.

Presidents Bush and Obama executed these rules throughout their presidencies, and so now, we remove more people in a single year than we used to in ten-year periods. Obama was removing over four hundred thousand persons per year, until it dawned on him that the Republicans in Congress were never going to approve comprehensive immigration reform, as they'd once promised earlier in his presidency. "You enforce the law, and then we'll talk comprehensive reform," they said. They never got to that second clause, and so Obama felt emboldened to do "reform" anyway, through DACA[1] and then DAPA.[2] He retained an emphasis on criminal deportations, however, and so the United States still deports hundreds of thousands of people each year, even for non-violent crimes.

This mass deportation system has resulted in strange American diasporas: In Mexico, Guatemala, and El Salvador, the arrival of so many deportees from the United States has exacerbated social and economic problems that were already terrible.[3] What happens to a society, any society, let alone those torn apart by civil war, when tens of thousands of people with criminal records arrive every year? What if a small fraction really *are* violent and quite horrible, and what if they are members of criminal gangs that, thanks to American deportation policy, are now transnational? Daniel Kanstroom, Tanya Golash-Boza, and several other scholars have given thick accounts of how American deportation policy has undermined fragile societies, even as it's not obvious how these policies have "helped" the United States. In one area, namely drug trafficking, we seem to have provided an unusual labor force for international criminal organizations interested in selling and distributing drugs in the United States.

Deportation policy is one area of immigration law where a straight nationalist approach doesn't work, while also being immoral. We still spend billions on our criminal justice systems, but Americans also consume illicit drugs at a rapid clip, and small planes, sophisticated submarines, and tunnels can simply bypass a "big, beautiful wall," even

---

[1] https://en.wikipedia.org/wiki/Deferred_Action_for_Childhood_Arrivals.
[2] https://en.wikipedia.org/wiki/Deferred_Action_for_Parents_of_Americans.
[3] https://www.americanprogress.org/issues/immigration/news/2017/10/20/440400/tps-holders-are-integral-members-of-the-u-s-economy-and-society/.

if we do spend billions to build such a thing. By destabilizing societies to the south of us, we almost guarantee that more people will also attempt to cross here, if just to avoid the chaos and violence in San Salvador or in Guatemala City. And in the last two decades, as we remove more immigrants, many of whom have deep family and community connections, we've caused untold misery to people who aren't so different from American citizens. Many people have been removed for drug offenses, for instance, and yet how many college students and professors do I know, all of them American citizens, who use drugs or even have minor drug offenses? When the law treats people with similar offenses in radically different ways, based solely on status, the present law evokes the worst of laws past.

Many scholars and practitioners and even law enforcement officials have criticized federal deportation policy. They've called for restoring common forms of relief, as when the removal of an immigrant will have a clear negative impact on his family and community, or when it seems disproportionate to his offense. Some law enforcement officials and prosecutors have changed their practices to drop or reduce criminal charges in cases where a defendant might also face deportation, thus behaving as though mindful of federal immigration consequences that can arise from local criminal prosecutions. And in many instances, jurisdictions have said that they will not cooperate with federal authorities as they pursue deportations. Proponents of "sanctuary cities" tend to agree that deportation policies have gone too far, and they've moved to protect their residents from that system.

Kevin R. Johnson

In 1996, Congress passed immigration reform legislation that has had dramatic impacts. Among other things, the reforms expanded crime-based removals and created a new system of "expedited removal," which might better be described as summary deportation with few protections for non-citizens. The Trump administration proposes to use both tools in pursuit of its aggressive immigration enforcement agenda and the impacts will be pernicious.

a) The racial impacts of expanded crime-based removals.

Crime-based removals, as expanded in 1996, are the centerpiece of contemporary immigration enforcement. The Obama administration prioritized the removal of "criminal aliens." Ramping up immigration enforcement by focusing on the criminal justice pipeline for removals proved to be an efficient strategy. Immigrants in jail are not hard to find. Moreover, removing criminals raises far fewer civil rights concerns than, for example, locating and removing undocumented workers through the use of workplace raids,[1] with employers as well as workers protesting Importantly, immigrants with criminal histories have few political defenders. Opposition to their removal is not nearly as great as popular resistance to removing other groups of immigrants, such as undocumented college students.[2]

With the 1996 immigration reforms expanding crime-based removals, the Obama administration refined programs that allowed state criminal justice systems to directly feed immigrants into the federal immigration removal system. Such refinements made it possible for President Obama to set a series of removal records.[3] Some[4] years saw the removal of as many as four hundred thousand non-citizens, including lawful permanent residents, from the United States. During the eight years of his presidency, more than two and a half million non-citizens were deported—more than during any other U.S. presidency. Immigration and Customs Enforcement data[5] show that, in fiscal year 2016, crime-based removals represented more than ninety percent of the non-citizens removed from the interior of the United States.

The U.S. criminal justice system is notorious for producing racially disparate results. African Americans and Latinos continue to be

---

[1] https://theconversation.com/how-trumps-immigration-enforcement-could-affect-families-and-communities-69019.

[2] https://www.theatlantic.com/education/archive/2015/01/why-us-colleges-should-welcome-undocumented-immigrants/385049/.

[3] http://abcnews.go.com/Politics/obamas-deportation-policy-numbers/story?id=41715661.

[4] http://www.pewresearch.org/fact-tank/2016/12/16/u-s-immigrant-deportations-fall-to-lowest-level-since-2007/.

[5] https://www.ice.gov/removal-statistics/2016.

disproportionately arrested and incarcerated as they have been throughout U.S. history, as described in Michelle Alexander's influential book *The New Jim Crow: Mass Incarceration in the Age of Colorblindedness* (2010). As a result of focusing removal efforts on "criminal aliens,"[1] the U.S. immigrant removal system has yielded similarly unequal results.

Consequently, increases in crime-based removals under President Obama resulted in the removal of a disproportionate number of Latino immigrants. Today, more than ninety-five percent of removals in the United States are of Latino non-citizens, despite the fact that the total immigrant population in the United States is much more diverse. Latino immigrants comprise only about fifty percent of lawful immigrants, and around seventy percent of undocumented ones.

Donald Trump began his presidential campaign by claiming that Mexico was sending its criminals to the United States, and promised to deport Mexican immigrants en masse. Two executive orders issued on January 25, 2017 demonstrate that the Trump administration plans to expand on the Obama administration's focus on removing "criminal aliens." President Trump's executive orders will likely have devastating impacts in terms of crime-based immigrant removals. They expand the non-citizens who will be the targets of immigration enforcement efforts and will likely continue to have disparate racial impacts on Latinos.

b) Expanded expedited removals.

The 1996 immigration reforms created what is referred to as "expedited removal." Under that procedure, an Immigration and Customs Enforcement (ICE) officer may order an individual removed from the United States without a hearing or further review, if the officer determines that the individual is inadmissible to the United States for fraud or misrepresentation or does not have a valid visa/entry document.

---

[1] https://casetext.com/posts/doubling-down-on-racial-discrimination-the-racially-disparate-impacts-of-crimmigration-law#!.

Since created in 1996, expedited removal—and its abbreviated procedures and unreviewable decisions—had been limited to non-citizens (1) apprehended within one hundred miles of the U.S. border; and (2) in the country for less than fourteen days. Persons close to the border for such a short period of time are likely to have fewer ties to the United States than longer-term residents. One of President Trump's immigration executive orders expands expedited removal. It eliminates the geographic limits to expedited removal and makes the summary procedures applicable to non-citizens in the country for as long as two years. Summary deportations of persons, including those with ties to the United States and family (including U.S. citizen children), friends, community, and a job, raise glaring Due Process red flags. Once the Trump administration seeks to implement the executive order, we are likely to see lawsuits challenging the constitutionality of the expanded expedited removal procedures.

President Trump will not likely focus expedited removal on particular racial or religious groups or nationalities. However, such removals almost certainly will have disparate impacts on non-citizens from Mexico and Central America, who often are profiled as undocumented immigrants and comprise a large portion of the undocumented population.

David Brotherton

In 1997, the first year this legislation was in effect, there were nearly one hundred and fifteen thousand removals and the next year this increased to around one hundred and seventy-five thousand. By the end of Clinton's presidency, the man who pledged to end welfare as we knew it also ended immigration as we knew it and banished to their homelands nearly nine hundred thousand persons. Bush went further still, forcibly removing over two million immigrant residents during his two terms, and by the time President Obama finished his fifth year in office he had taken the art of banishment to the next level,

---

[1]https://en.wikipedia.org/wiki/Antiterrorism_and_Effective_Death_Penalty_Act_of_1996.

equaling Bush's achievement in three years less. The legislation, aided and abetted by the Patriot Act of 2001 and the Anti-Terrorism and Effective Death Penalty Act (AEDPA)[1] of 1996, has created a deportation juggernaut with Congress further burnishing its anti-immigrant credentials by mandating the Department of Homeland Security through its Immigration apparatus (i.e., the Department of Immigration and Customs Enforcement) to fill the detention camps with thirty-four thousand detainees daily. It is the only federal department to have such human quotas placed upon it.

Thus, these laws are incredibly punitive, vindictive, and irrational. For example, people can be placed in removal proceedings based on crimes they committed in the past and for which they were duly sentenced. Hence deportation can be viewed as a form of double jeopardy in many cases. Also, since deportation is considered an administrative action rather than an act of punishment, the law does not require that "deportable aliens" be provided with legal representation. Further, the crimes for which someone is deported, often referred to as "aggravated felonies," vary from the passing of bad checks to homicide. Clearly the extreme consequence of permanent removal for crimes which are, in many cases, quite minor, is wildly disproportionate with levels of social, psychological, and economic harm both to the deportee and to his or her family of unimaginable proportions. Finally, we need to think of the broader repercussions to entire societies created by these mass expulsions, particular those countries with few resources and weak state structures, e.g. the countries of Central America that currently boast the highest rates of homicide in the world, in part caused by the floods of deportees who brought with them their gang subcultures learned in the U.S.

Certainly, Trump will be able to process more cases of expedited removals as his executive orders change the priorities for ICE and its agents and makes any offense in the past committed by a non-citizen a reason for deportation rather than the so-called "violent criminals" that Obama had said should be the main focus of the country's deportation regime.

The states acting benevolently on immigration.

Can the states counter some of the existing anti-immigrant federal legislation on the books, or even potentially stall or prevent implementation of further restrictionist executive orders by the Trump administration? If Arizona and other states can pass anti-immigrant legislation, why can't individual states go in the other direction and pass legislation favorable to immigrants, granting them full rights? Is this realistic, and how do you envision such a prospect coming about?

John S.W. Park

Several scholars have studied state and local responses to federal immigration law over the past two decades, and they say that most of the states and local jurisdictions have moved to *support* federal rules, not so much to limit them. Virginia, Georgia, and South Carolina do not allow students who are out of status to matriculate at the public colleges and universities, for example, and cities like Escondido, California, and Hazelton, Pennsylvania, have passed rules prohibiting landlords from renting to anyone who cannot prove lawful immigration status. Costa Mesa, a city in Orange County, declared itself a "rule of law" community in 2010—in a resolution, the city suggested that local law enforcement officials should "check for papers" even in routine stops, and then remand persons suspected of being out of status to the proper immigration authorities. Federal policies approved by President Bush in 2008 encouraged local police cooperation: Under the Secure Communities[1] program, local jurisdictions could receive federal resources and training if they agreed to participate in immigration enforcement. Costa Mesa was among several dozen cities that were participating by 2010.

But Santa Ana is maybe twenty minutes away from Costa Mesa by car, and Santa Ana has moved in the opposite direction. The city's

---

[1] https://en.wikipedia.org/wiki/Secure_Communities.

police force tended only to collaborate with federal immigration authorities in cases of violent crime—in other respects, public officials tended to be deliberately inattentive to immigration status when considering requests for city services, police protection, and even public employment for the city. Many residents of the city did not have legal status, and yet they attended and participated in city council meetings, on school boards, and in other public settings. After the 2016 election, Santa Ana passed a resolution calling itself a "sanctuary city," as if to defy the new President.

Santa Ana was part of a larger state-wide trend, perhaps exemplified best in California's Trust Act,[1] signed by Governor Jerry Brown in 2013. That state rule directed state and local officials not to hold immigrants facing deportation in state and local facilities, unless federal officials offered proof that the person being held was *already* convicted of a deportable crime. Democrats controlled the state, and they were more sympathetic to the Santa Anas than the Costa Mesas. President Trump, though, spoke in Costa Mesa during his campaign, vowing to crack down on illegal immigration, to build that wall, and to withhold federal funds from cities that did not help federal immigration officials or that otherwise provided "sanctuary" to illegal immigrants.

In other contexts, I've argued that the last time that some states and local jurisdictions were so at odds with the federal government about a "removal" policy was during the nineteenth century. This was when fugitive slaves were running north, when some northern jurisdictions moved to protect them, and when southerners passed stringent rules designed to help them "recover their property." I've reminded my own students that the underground railroad was a form of resistance to slavery during a time when slavery was *legal*, when black people *were* property, and when the constitution and several federal laws protected white property owners to recover "their people." George Washington, Thomas Jefferson, and Andrew Jackson had all posted ads in popular newspapers that described their fugitive slaves, and as presidents, they signed or supported rules favoring white slave owners. Andrew Jackson and Roger Taney both

---

[1] http://www.catrustact.org/.

owned many slaves. Levi Coffin, Harriet Tubman, the students and faculty at Oberlin College—they *assisted* runaway slaves, however, and they encouraged others to break the law, even if that meant jail or murder for them, or a civil war to purge the nation of slavery.

It's hard to say whether President Trump will pass his own version of the Fugitive Slave Act[1] of 1850, that infamous rule that punished state and local officials for failing to detain runaway slaves and to assist slave owners. The Act insisted that "all good citizens" had an obligation to help masters locate their slaves. Citizens who helped runaway slaves could be punished, too; they were not "good citizens." One can imagine a President Trump and his Republican Congress passing a set of rules that require us to assist in the removal of undocumented persons, no matter the length of their residency here or the depth of their connections. Before we comply, we should study our own history, to give us clues as to how best to consider our own dilemmas.

The past is not even past: President Trump has re-hung, in the Oval Office, just to the left of his desk, a portrait of Andrew Jackson. And yet even during his presidency, the twenty dollar bill will have a new face—Harriet Tubman's—a change approved under President Obama's administration. I'd recommend that Americans take a good long look at the new face of the twenty dollar bill, then also consider President Trump's own heroes, and then think hard about which side of history seems most pleasing and inspiring for our own future.

Kevin R. Johnson

On the one hand, the U.S. government decides which non-citizens to admit to, and deport from, the United States. Congress has passed a comprehensive immigration law, the Immigration and Nationality Act, which regulates immigration. On the other hand, the states are the primary enforcers of the criminal laws and otherwise are responsible for integrating non-citizen residents into the community. The legitimacy of the conventional demarcation of sovereign powers between the federal and state governments can be seen in Supreme

---

[1] http://www.history.com/topics/black-history/fugitive-slave-acts.

Court decisions, such as *Arizona v. United States*[1] (2012) in which the Court struck down central provisions of an Arizona law that intruded on the federal powers to enforce the immigration laws.

Room exists for state and local governments to work with the U.S. government in federal immigration enforcement. However, the U.S. government must consent to state and local assistance. In addition, state governments have sovereign powers that cannot be infringed upon by the U.S. government in efforts to compel cooperation with immigration enforcement efforts. In the exercise of their police powers, some states have exercised their lawmaking power to improve the access of undocumented immigrants to public higher education, foster immigrant trust in local law enforcement offices, and otherwise seek to integrate immigrants into the community.

In recent times, the lines between the state, local, and federal governments in immigration enforcement have become blurred. Under a program called Secure Communities[2] which President Obama dismantled, state and local law enforcement agencies shared arrest information with federal immigration authorities, and detained immigrant criminal offenders. Criminal offenders were then taken into custody by federal immigration authorities.

Complaints had been registered that Secure Communities was overbroad and subjected minor criminal offenders to removal. In November 2014, the Obama administration responded to the criticism and replaced Secure Communities with the Priority Enforcement Program (PEP),[3] which was narrower in scope. In bringing back Service Communities in one of his Executive Orders, President Trump dismantled PEP and expanded the scope of crime-based removals.

In addition, the Trump administration in a January 25 Executive Order has sought to mandate state and local assistance in federal immigration enforcement by threatening to eliminate federal funding to "sanctuary cities."[4] Trump's threat to defund such cities would

---

[1] https://www.law.cornell.edu/supremecourt/text/11-182.

[2] https://www.ice.gov/secure-communities.

[3] https://www.ice.gov/pep.

[4] https://theconversation.com/whats-the-history-of-sanctuary-spaces-and-why-do-they-matter-69100.

seem to require congressional authorization.[1] In addition, the Executive Order fails to define "sanctuary cities." If Congress were to pass legislation defunding "sanctuary cities," state and local governments may challenge the law as infringing on the sovereign powers of the states.

Efforts by the U.S. government to compel cities to cooperate in federal immigration enforcement efforts are already encountering formidable resistance. The California legislature is preparing a game plan, including the retention of former Attorney General Eric Holder, for a showdown with the Trump administration on immigration enforcement.[2] Legislators have proposed legislation, for example, which would limit state information sharing about immigrants with the federal government.

It is important to recognize the important state and local criminal law enforcement concerns at stake in their cooperation with federal immigration enforcement. Some state and local law enforcement leaders worry that immigrants lose trust in local police when they are perceived to be deeply involved in federal immigration enforcement. Loss of trust, in turn, can reduce the willingness of immigrants to help authorities combat crime and undermine state and local law enforcement efforts.[3] Local police need the cooperation of all people in the community, including lawful and undocumented immigrants, in reporting crime and aiding criminal prosecutions. To that end, the Los Angeles Police Department's Special Order 40 limits police inquiry into the immigration status of crime victims, witnesses, and suspects.[4] The separation of criminal law enforcement from federal immigration enforcement is consistent with the Supreme Court's finding in *Arizona v. United States*[5] (2012) that the federal government has the authority

---

[1] http://www.politifact.com/truth-o-meter/statements/2016/dec/01/bill-de-blasio/new-york-city-mayor-says-president-cant-defund-san/.

[2] http://sd24.senate.ca.gov/news/2016-12-05-california-legislature-takes-immediate-action-protect-immigrant-communities.

[3] http://www.policylink.org/sites/default/files/INSECURE_COMMUNITIES_REPORT_FINAL.PDF.

[4] http://assets.lapdonline.org/assets/pdf/SO_40.pdf.

[5] https://www.oyez.org/cases/2011/11-182.

to admit and remove immigrants, with ordinary law enforcement primarily in the hands of local law enforcement agencies.

To foster state and local cooperation with federal immigration enforcement, one of President Trump's January 25 Executive Orders[1] brings back "287 agreements"—authorized by Immigration and Nationality Act 287(g)—between state and local governments and the federal government to enforce the immigration laws. Such agreements had been largely abandoned by the Obama administration.

The civil rights impacts of local police involvement in immigration enforcement are an issue of concern. A federal court in 2015 found that the Maricopa County Sheriff's Office in Arizona, in the guise of assisting federal immigration enforcement, had engaged in a pattern and practice of racial discrimination against Latinos, U.S. citizens as well as immigrants.[2] These civil rights abuses show the potential costs of state and local law enforcement assistance in federal immigration enforcement efforts. The same risks will exist for the Trump administration as it enlists state and local law enforcement cooperation in immigration enforcement.

David Brotherton

It's very difficult for states to do anything other than establish sanctuary cities that will prevent local police collaborating with ICE. ICE is an extremely powerful national police force and can operate anywhere with few restrictions. Essentially, we have allowed ICE to develop with few constraints and little oversight and this has happened under both Bush and Obama and has been given even more legal powers and budgetary increases under Trump. For the past two decades the deportation-industrial complex has been allowed to grow almost unhindered and now we are paying an enormous price both socially and politically. If the states refuse to work with ICE, particularly over the application of 287g, which seeks to have local police forces partner with ICE agents, then it sets up a conflict between the powers of the federal government and those of the states and certainly under the Trump administration it is difficult to see how the states could mount a successful defense of their residents. However, this is not to say that they should not try or that immigrants' rights advocates should not do everything possible to expose the invasive and destructive practices of this agency and its threat to democracy and human rights.

The worst anomalies of our immigration system.

What are the failures of our immigration system that most worry you? What anomalies in recent court decisions toward the rights of immigrants are least understood by the general public? Should we do away with detention for immigrants altogether? Where in this country have you seen signs of movement in a pro-human rights direction that people need to be more aware of?

John S.W. Park

In a forthcoming book and in other venues, I've argued that immigration law and national sovereignty have shown symptoms of much deeper problems, problems rooted in modernity itself. We're living through two ongoing revolutions, in communications technologies and in transportation technologies. The first allows us to see one another across vast distances much more than ever before; the second allows people to fling themselves here and there much faster and further, too. Imagine the United States in 1800—no Panama Canal, no telephone or telegraph, no steam engines, and certainly no airports. I once had to persuade my own children that there was once no internet or cell phones when I was a bitty kid, that Instagram is a really new thing.

These changes have become a part of our lives, they're a part of the world now, even in some of the most poor, most desperate, and most chaotic places on the planet. When people there "see," through their own televisions and mobile devices, that they can maybe go to Europe or parts of Asia or the United States, and then live decent, relatively comfortable lives, they're going to want to leave. Their arrival in large numbers is the result of very, very large numbers: nearly a third of the world's population lives in places that are food insecure, politically dysfunctional, or otherwise falling apart, and so even when a small fraction of those folks migrate, they're soon very visible in countries that don't want them. No wall, fence, or other heinous barrier will likely change the underlying math that causes so much unwanted movement and human suffering. Unless we tend to conditions *outside* our boundaries—to work with others to create just, stable societies—we will feel overwhelmed, and we will fall prey to those who offer easy answers and empty promises.

Thinking beyond ourselves and our boundaries—this has precedence, too, and we should learn from that history. In the ashes of World War II, for its own strategic interests and for humanitarian reasons, the United States did not punish the "losers," Italy, Japan and Nazi Germany. Instead, the United States worked with allies there, floated giant loans and grants for reconstruction, and developed thick ties to these former adversaries. Now, we don't have large populations of illegal Japanese or illegal Germans living in the United States, people who are fleeing their own countries, because the United States itself helped to make Japan and Germany more livable.

Thus, instead of criticizing Mexico or other sending countries, the United States ought to work with its partners and other wealthier nations to develop decent, just societies in these places, and to create circumstances where the people there will not see a need to leave their homes. Americans should fess up to policies that may have made things worse. Americans should quit taking drugs, or they should at least consider how a single line of cocaine, multiplied millions of times, can cause misery far away from where they're getting high. Instead of making conditions worse, through our foreign policy or through thousands of acts of carelessness, Americans should try harder to make things better for everyone, everywhere. That is when we are best, when we show, through our own example, a willingness to sacrifice and to assist people who aren't just like us.

We should acknowledge and cope with a much smaller world, where we can see and be with one another ever more easily than before. Many other problems reflect this new reality: Pollution in one country, for instance, can become a problem for every country. Despite the skeptics, I and you and everyone really should be concerned about coal plants outside Beijing, because their contribution to carbon levels will screw up the climate in Santa Barbara. The weather in Santa Barbara is spectacular, and so if I love it, I should care about pollution in China and in India and in the United States, too, as this is part of my own enlightened self-interest. And aside from just self-interest, seeing children, much like my own children, suffering from more direct forms of pollution in Beijing and in Delhi is simply heartbreaking, so much so that we should wish and work for another world where no kid is trapped indoors because the air is toxic. My child is not somehow more entitled to clean air than another child.

That whole cliché about injustice anywhere being a threat to justice everywhere—that's actually profound and wise and right. To put your own nation and your own people first, to build walls, and to cut off and to disengage—it's self-defeating, it simply isn't going to work, and it's ill-suited to our interconnected world.

Kevin R. Johnson

As discussed above, crime-based removals, and their disparate racial impacts, are a problem with modern removals that should be addressed. The use of detention in immigration enforcement implicates similar concerns. President Donald Trump has set in motion efforts to ramp up immigrant detention.[1] His executive order on border security and immigration promises to increase the use of the detention of immigrants while they await removal hearings and removal from the United States.[2] Trump's order announces the end of "catch and release" of undocumented immigrants after their apprehension. Historically, unless found to pose a public safety or flight risk, non-citizens have been allowed to post a bond and be

---

[1] https://theconversation.com/trumps-immigration-policies-will-pick-up-where-obamas-left-off-70187.

[2] https://www.whitehouse.gov/presidential-actions/executive-order-border-security-immigration-enforcement-improvements/.

released from custody while their removal proceedings moved forward.

Detention has long been a tool in the arsenal of the U.S. government in immigration enforcement. It goes at least as far back as the detention of Chinese immigrants on Angel Island in San Francisco Bay, which began processing immigrants in the late 1800s.[1] Detention of immigrants as a method of immigration enforcement saw an upswing at the tail-end of the twentieth century. In the 1980s, for example, the Reagan administration employed detention to discourage Central Americans, thousands of whom were fleeing civil wars, from migrating to the United States. Several U.S. presidents responded to mass migrations of Cubans in the 1980s,[2] who came in the Mariel boatlift, and Haitians fleeing political violence in the 1980s and 1990s, with detention.

The Obama administration generally allowed for noncitizens to bond out of custody while their removal proceedings were pending. But it also employed immigrant detention liberally in some instances, including the mass detention of Central American families.

Just as old as immigrant detention are legal challenges to immigrant detention. One of those suits, *Orantes-Hernandez v. Thornburgh*[3] (1990), was a class action brought against the U.S. government by asylum applicants from El Salvador. The asylum applicants challenged the mass detention of Salvadoran asylum seekers and various policies that violated their right to counsel. The court found that the U.S. government had been transferring asylum seekers from major urban areas where they could readily secure counsel to detention in remote locations where they could not. The U.S. Court of Appeals for the Ninth Circuit affirmed an injunction barring the U.S. government from restricting access to counsel.

Despite many successful challenges, the use of detention in immigration enforcement increased with the immigration reforms of 1996.[4] Immigrant detention continues to be criticized—and litigated.

---

[1] https://www.npr.org/templates/story/story.php?storyId=130380169.

[2] http://caselaw.findlaw.com/us-9th-circuit/1146031.html.

[3] https://openjurist.org/919/f2d/549/orantes-hernandez-v-thornburgh.

[4] https://www.amazon.com/American-Gulag-Inside-Immigration-Prisons/dp/0520246691.

In *Jennings v. Rodriguez*,[1] the Supreme Court currently has before it a class action raising the question whether immigrants, like virtually all U.S. citizens placed in criminal and civil detention, must be guaranteed a bond hearing and possible release from custody. Similarly, in response to an increase in women and children fleeing widespread violence in Central America, the Obama administration began detaining thousands of unaccompanied minors and entire families. In *Flores v. Lynch*[2] in 2016, the Ninth Circuit found that the detention of Central American minors violated a settlement agreement.

The long history of detention has an equally long history of legal challenges. These challenges will likely continue during the Trump years, with the President making detention a cornerstone of his immigration enforcement plans.

David Brotherton

There are numerous threats to immigrants which are probably some of the most severe since the Second World War. The vast majority of undocumented immigrants are not engaged in criminal activities and should not be penalized for wanting to reside in this country. In fact, first-generation immigrants be they legal or undocumented are the population with the least connection to criminal activity of anyone. But this doesn't stop Trump from saying the exact opposite, and, of course, this is in line with his basic philosophy that objective reality and "facts" should not be taken seriously if they conflict with his ideological goals. Yes, the detention camps should be shut down, the raft of anti-immigrant laws should be abandoned, and a whole new set of laws should be developed that give undocumented immigrants a pathway to legality.

Right now we have allowed the development of a vast population of American children who grow up without one or both parents lost

---

[1] http://www.scotusblog.com/case-files/cases/jennings-v-rodriguez/.

[2] https://scholar.google.com/scholar_case?case=12780774456837741811&hl=en& as_sdt=6&as_vis=1&oi=scholarre=12780774456837741811&hl=en&as_sdt=6&as _vis=1&oi=scholarr.

to the deportation process. Further, around the world we now have a new diaspora of millions of displaced people all of whom were in some way socialized by the United States, many of them with permanent family links to this country that can never be restored. The U.S. has become the world's number one deportation nation responsible for massive levels of family fragmentation and global destabilization. These policies have no place in a so-called civilized society that boasts of its adherence to democratic principles.

Consequently, we have to ask ourselves what kind of society have we become? Given that we were one of the major signatories to the U.N. Declaration of Human Rights in 1948, following the genocidal crimes of fascism and the extraordinary social destruction associated with World War II, it is both tragic and ironic that we are now one of the biggest transgressors of this historic agreement as we turn refugees and immigrants into the despised and unwanted Other. We must hope that the U.S. can get beyond this present dark phase of its development. The next couple of years will see to what extent we prize democracy and social solidarity over the reactionary impulses that have been unleashed by years of punishing neoliberal policies meted out to the majority of U.S. residents.

From Immigrant Rights to Human Rights:
A Radical Reconceptualization Beyond
Left and Right

"Whether immigration laws have been crude or cruel, whether they may have reflected xenophobia in general or anti-Semitism or anti-Catholicism, the responsibility belongs to Congress." — Justice Felix Frankfurter, *Harisiades v. Shaughnessy* (1952)

"I [Mr. Delgado, Dominican-born resident of Manhattan for twenty-seven years] want to tell you [the judge at the deportation hearing] and my family that I am no thief. I've never taken anything from anyone in my life, not even a pair of nail clippers. What happened to me was wrong. It was a miscarriage of justice. I agreed to a plea for something I didn't do. I thought I was gonna get a short sentence and then be released. I thought if I didn't do that I was gonna get fifteen years. That's what they threatened me with. No one told me I was gonna get this [deportation]. Okay, I have a temper and I can get violent. It happens when I drink, and I'd been drinking when all this happened. I don't remember much about it, except the guy gets the better of me and I go home. That's about it. But I didn't steal nothing from nobody. All I wanted to be was a baseball player, that's all. I got a scholarship to some university, but it didn't work out. I didn't get picked up, and so I got depressed. I get very depressed and I start to drink. I know I need treatment for this, but I don't need jail and I don't need to be torn away from everything I love. This is my life here. I've been here since I was a kid. This is all I know. Here's my family right here. I don't have no family where you wanna send me. What am I gonna do there? Where am I gonna live? How am I gonna see my children again? Where's the justice in all of this?" — quoted in David C. Brotherton, "Exiling New Yorkers," in *Keeping Out the Other: A Critical Introduction to Immigration Enforcement Today* (2008)

The Nature of the Immigration "Problem."

The contemporary manifestation of the immigration crisis, in full flow now for more than twenty years, is better understood as a moral panic, rather than a typical policy problem amenable to rational solutions. The kind of moral panic toward immigration we have been witnessing in this country for so long is really a rechanneling of economic anxiety, stemming from the crisis of globalization, toward the vulnerable bodies of immigrants, since we as a nation have felt ourselves helpless to do anything about globalization. The fact that the moral panic often reaches crescendos independent of the magnitude of the problem (such as the Prop. 187 movement in California in the early 1990s when NAFTA had barely taken off, or the current anxiety when net immigration from Mexico is declining and probably negative)[1] suggests that the hysteria is often disconnected from reality.

Although Donald Trump's executive orders so far might sound unprecedented, in fact every initiative he has taken or proposes to take has plenty of precedent in our immigration history, in all three branches of government. Our federal immigration policy began about a hundred and twenty-five years ago in an exclusivist and racist vein, targeting the Chinese, then the Japanese and other Asians, and after that southern and eastern Europeans, before moving on to Mexicans as the prime target of exclusion for about one hundred years, where we remain today with the recent addition of Muslims and Arabs as special targets.

The judicial branch has historically granted the executive great leeway to do as it wishes on immigration, considering it (quite wrongly, I think) an arena of foreign policy, passing under what's known as the "plenary powers" doctrine. Though there have been times, in periods of liberal ascendancy, when there has been pushback against plenary power, the idea is inherently connected to the way federal immigration policy came into being and was conceptualized in the early going, so it is difficult to get away from. If the judicial branch, in the wake of the Trump administration's expected assault on immigration, takes a restraining posture, it would actually be a deviance from, rather than a continuation of, historical precedence.

We have come to an impasse at last, after a century and a quarter of misguided federal immigration policy, where there is no way out of

---

[1] http://www.pewhispanic.org/2015/11/19/more-mexicans-leaving-than-coming-to-the-u-s/.

our current moral panic but to recognize the immigration crisis as a human rights catastrophe of historic proportions, ranking up there with the greatest known tragedies toward mass populations, and to address it as such rather than resting hope in any of the so-called "reform" measures that do not get to the bottom of the human rights tragedy.

"Comprehensive immigration reform," as it's called, has been nothing but deceitful in any of the various forms it has kept appearing in for the last thirty-five years, because it exacerbates, rather than alleviates, the human rights dimension of the present crisis. Similarly, the current misguided focus on saving the so-called "Dreamers" (people who arrived at a young age) is nothing but a brilliant tactical maneuver to split off the "good" from the "bad" immigrants, thereby compromising the human rights stature of the entire immigrant population, extending even into legal residents and naturalized citizens when the full consequences of the disciplinary mechanisms trained on immigrants as a result of the Dreamer logic are taken into account. The alleged "legal" versus "illegal" immigrant separation, which restrictionists are so fond of using, is a complete myth, given the way our immigration system works, and is designed to strike a blow at the human rights to which all immigrants should be fully entitled.

The Trump administration is only carrying to its logical conclusion the fatal contradiction in our immigration laws, which is that the deportee is not granted the rights accruing to criminals because deportation is considered a civil or administrative matter rather than a criminal one, despite the fact that deportation has vast consequences on human lives, as severe as the harshest criminal proceedings.

The logical way to address this fissure, which is now manifesting in the tragic mass deportation policy Trump has just embarked on, would be to make deportation a criminal matter, so that the entire range of constitutional rights comes into play. Otherwise the immigrant is prosecuted as a criminal but is deprived of the rights of a criminal defendant; either deportation is or is not criminal, it cannot be treated as if it were criminal from the government's point of view but not as if it were criminal from the immigrant's point of view.

Immigration, in short, should be removed from criminality, even in the face of any "violations." It is actually an administrative matter, as it has been and should be, and the concessions to criminal disciplinary action made by neoliberal policymakers over the last quarter century in particular should give way to a regime where there is never detention on purely immigration-related charges, where we start moving toward completely free and open borders (NAFTA, in the greatest anomaly contributing to the creation of the "illegal" immigrant population, removed restrictions on capital movement in North America at the same time as it clamped down on labor movement and generated multiple channels for "illegality"), and where we recognize that the neoliberal elites are responsible for a general punitive regime that is targeted not just toward immigrants but toward poor people in general.

The year 1996 seems in retrospect to be the true turning point in our recent constitutional history, as anti-immigrant, anti-welfare, and anti-terrorist legislation was passed in the same year, with mutually reinforcing effects sending shock waves that reverberate throughout the polity to this day. With the proliferation of new categories and exceptions, half a million elderly and disabled immigrants lost SSI, while another million immigrants lost food stamps; at the same time, new descriptions of crimes were created to pull together immigrants and terrorists in a haze of disrepute that has never cleared up.

It should also be recognized that there is *no* moral right to exclude, and that all the philosophical reasonings for exclusion (based on national sovereignty) are on very thin ground indeed. If globalization is going to work, then discarding the false grounds for exclusion is the only way to go about it. Given the technological capacity in the hands of the state, exclusion inevitably turns into a process whereby the human rights of the native population are truncated, and national sovereignty turns into a monstrous idea that soon ends up having little to do with protecting borders and everything to do with reigning in human rights for everyone.

As Trump moves forward aggressively on his stated racist agenda, we need to have our baseline moral argument straight, to counter the clarity of the racists in power, and our starting point should be this:

As soon as a person steps foot in America, he or she has full constitutional rights, without any exceptions.

Certainly, the longer one is present on American soil, the claim to constitutional rights, including an absolute bar against deportation, becomes stronger and stronger, but the claim to rights should not have anything to do with length of stay; setting up arbitrary cut-off points means that they will always be subject to political whims, extending further and further against the moral logic of membership due to one's presence alone. At the moment Trump is claiming expedited removals, i.e. deportation without judicial hearings, a concept that was enshrined in the 1996 legislation called the Illegal Immigration Reform and Immigrant Responsibility Act (IIRIRA), for those present in the U.S. for less than two years.

Our ongoing violation of the rights of long-term immigrants in particular is at par with the history of some of the worst crimes against humanity, given the size and nature of the resident population (about ten million people, multiplied by their immediate families, so we are talking about perhaps fifty million people directly affected, inhabiting all sorts of mixed-status families). Unless we treat the problem in this true perspective, any short-sighted policy solutions will only make the problem worse and the stain on our constitutional order will get all the worse.

Immigration before federalization.

Until the 1880s, when the federal immigration bureaucracy came into being for the first time, immigration was a state issue, with different states treating immigrants differently, depending on economic and social conditions. In the generally laissez-faire environment that prevailed from the founding of the nation until one hundred years later, there was not even a systematic method for knowing how many immigrants had arrived. Immigrants, who were not yet naturalized, could vote in elections. There was some enforcement by the states of the "liable to become a public charge" (LPC) principle,[1] but before federal laws made much of this idea there was considerable laxity

---

[1] https://en.wikipedia.org/wiki/Liable_to_become_a_Public_Charge_(LPC).

about this rule. Whereas contemporary immigration law, especially since the passage of the Immigration and Nationality Act (INA) of 1965, gives much lip service to family unification as a principle,[1] in reality it was only during the era when immigration was not under federal control that family unification truly worked operationally.

All was not peaches and roses, however, even in the free environment—we might call it a condition very close to open borders—of the nineteenth century; successive movements of immigrants after the original English stock were each considered in exactly the same terms of approbation that we see today: That they were apt to be public charges, that they were unassimilable, that their cultural values were "un-American," that they were of inferior racial stock and carriers of disease, and that they would be disloyal to America and contribute to its democratic collapse. Such charges were leveled against the Germans (going back to Benjamin Franklin's castigation of that "stupid, swarthy" race), the Irish, and Catholics in general during the era when states held sway over immigration, the difference being that federal laws didn't exist then to subject the different European groups to systematic, nation-wide oppression.

Partly it was the existence of leeway amongst the states that made the continuation of the first truly anti-immigrant legislation, the Alien and Sedition Acts of 1798,[2] unsustainable; had there been a federal bureaucracy in existence at the beginning of the nineteenth century, we might never have experienced the open borders of that century, fueling the strongest sustained era of economic growth in history. The onset of federal immigration legislation was in response to increasing numbers of Chinese on the West Coast at the end of the century, which led to laws quickly rescinding immigration from Asia; it is worth pondering how dramatically America might have changed had immigration from Asia not been halted in the 1880s, only to be renewed almost a century later in 1965.

---

[1] http://www.history.com/topics/us-immigration-since-1965.
[2] https://www.loc.gov/rr/program/bib/ourdocs/Alien.html.

Immigration becomes a cover for racism in the late nineteenth and early twentieth centuries.

In a pattern that was to be repeated all through subsequent history, we actively encouraged the Chinese to migrate in large numbers when there were labor shortages, particularly to work on the railroads in the 1860s and 1870s. Once the need for labor was not so great, however, the presence of the Chinese created great racial resentment, which led to the Page Act of 1875,[1] the first attempt at federal immigration legislation, and then the Chinese Exclusion Act of 1882,[2] the first comprehensive federal legislation, which was clearly racist in intention. As for the Japanese, who started causing much anger on the West Coast with their acquisition of land and their agricultural skills, they were prevented from entering under the "Gentleman's Agreement" of 1907.[3] There was in fact an "Asiatic Barred Zone"[4] in effect from 1917 until the 1960s liberalization.

In a key decision upholding the Chinese Exclusion Act, namely *Chae Chan Ping v. United States* (1889), Justice Stephen Johnson Field wrote:

They remained strangers in the land, residing apart by themselves, and adhering to the customs and usages of their own country. It seemed impossible for them to assimilate with our people or to make any change in their habits or modes of living…. If, therefore, the government of the United States, through its legislative department, considers the presence of foreigners of a different race in this country, who will not assimilate with us, to be dangerous to its peace and security, their exclusion is not to be stayed because at the time there are no actual hostilities with the nation of which the foreigners are subjects.

The Chinese and Japanese who were already in the United States at the time of exclusion were forerunners of the current Latino population: Admitted but prevented from gaining citizenship, forced

---

[1] http://loveman.sdsu.edu/docs/1875Immigration%20Act.pdf.

[2] http://ocp.hul.harvard.edu/immigration/exclusion.html.

[3] https://www.britannica.com/event/Gentlemens-Agreement.

[4] http://encyclopedia.densho.org/Immigration%20Act%20of%201917/.

into a perpetual existence of what can only be called statelessness, stemming from American business's insistence on importing cheap labor from countries that were not desirable from the point of view of adding to the permanent roll of citizens.

It was in this period that the racial exclusion started going hand in hand with all sorts of exclusions that had not been on the books before, such as prostitutes, subversives (added after Leon Czolgosz's assassination of William McKinley, and persecuted especially during and after World War I, in consort with the FBI's vigorous pursuit of reds), and above all persons deemed LPC. American citizens who were female could not sponsor male non-citizens, though the same didn't apply in reverse. A Sikh named Bhagat Singh Thind tried during the 1920s to gain citizenship on the basis that Indians were Caucasians, but that didn't fly.[1]

These were the beginnings of a bureaucracy that has caused disaster after disaster. The logic of the exclusion of an entire racial group, Asians, led inexorably to the internment of Japanese Americans during World War II (had there been a federal bureaucracy that had existed during the peak of German immigration in the mid-nineteenth century, no doubt German Americans would have been in similar danger during World War I, but luckily for them they had already been accepted and had successfully assimilated during the course of the nineteenth century).

There is not a clear dividing line between exclusion (prevention of entry), deportation (exclusion after entry, these days going by the euphemism "removal"), and internment (entire racial groups put into actual or de facto custody, with strong similarities between Japanese internment and the various unregulated detention regimes that have followed in its wake, with currently more than forty thousand immigrants in federal detention at any given moment). The Jews, again a target of widespread prejudice before the passage of the national origins system in 1924, likewise paid a high price when refugees from the Nazi genocide were barred entry in the lead-up to and during World War II.

---

[1] http://www.bhagatsinghthind.com/legacy.html.

To empower a national immigration bureaucracy with resources is to let it use them against the most vulnerable segments of the population. Enforcement is always likely to pit one group against another and favor those who meet certain political criteria. The recent rapid assimilation of the "model minority," which since 1965 has turned out to be Asians, including South Asians, is the necessary counterpart to the prosecution of the political bias toward the unassimilable Mexicans, who are said to be loyal to their original homeland, the Southwestern United States (or Aztlán, to use the dismissive terminology deployed by white nationalists), rather than to America.

Once an immigration bureaucracy gets going, there are waves after waves of unintended consequences, all of which become inevitable when the principle of open borders is discarded.

For instance, the desire of the restrictionists in the last two decades of the nineteenth century and the first two decades of the twentieth century was to limit the unassimilable southern and eastern Europeans, which led to a series of attempts in these critical decades of incipient restrictionism to bar their entry. A number of legislative efforts, such as the implementation of literary tests in 1917 and 1921,[1] accomplished part of the goal, leading finally to complete success with the passage of the National Origins Act of 1924.[2] The Act went back to the 1890 census, rather than the later census, to calculate the numerical caps permitted to southern and eastern Europeans, in order to maximize the proportion of present and future northern and western Europeans.

But because labor needs had to be met somehow, American business was encouraged to seek Mexican immigration, and if this population didn't proceed on the path to naturalization, all the better for business. To prevent southern and eastern European immigration, America chose to import unauthorized Mexican immigrants for the duration of the twentieth century, occurring in successive bursts and

---

[1] https://www.smithsonianmag.com/history/how-america-grappled-immigration-100-years-ago-180962058/.
[2] http://historymatters.gmu.edu/d/5078.

leading to a population now considered infinitely less likely to assimilate by restrictionists.

Early in the twentieth century numerous commissions, such as the Dillingham Commission,[1] and numerous organizations, such as the Immigration Restriction League (IRL),[2] advocated restrictionist measures. These were the direct forerunners of such later organizations as the aforementioned Federation for American Immigration Reform (FAIR), the entity founded in the 1970s by environmentalist John Tanton, which has remained for the last forty years the leading anti-immigrant institutional force in this country, under the guise of various fronts such as the Center for Immigration Studies (CIS), NumbersUSA, etc., with Breitbart News a prime outlet for their supremacist views today.

The trend was set in the earlier era when progressives were often anti-immigrant, as was also true of labor unions. Although labor unions have at last accepted immigration, this has not been the case for much of their history. Progressivism, environmentalism, and trade unionism, in short, have often worked with eugenics ideology in the past to empower the federal immigration bureaucracy to embark on periodic assaults over groups out of political favor.

Though eugenics is no longer openly accepted, there is a strong taint of it in such polemics as Peter Brimelow's *Alien Nation* (1995), which, coming from a British immigrant himself, trades in many of eugenics' tropes, as is true of many other contemporary restrictionists. Brimelow calls for a return to a ninety percent majority white population, and this seems very much the agenda of Steve Bannon and other white supremacists in the White House today. Denial of automatic citizenship at birth, meaning the undoing of the Fourteenth Amendment, has been an explicit goal of restrictionists for a long time, and we are seeing efforts in this direction from the Trump administration as well.

When we endow a federal bureaucracy with unchecked authority, the distinctions between legal and illegal immigration become blurred, as law becomes malleable toward political ends, and a group

---

[1] http://ocp.hul.harvard.edu/immigration/dillingham.html.

[2] https://en.wikipedia.org/wiki/Immigration_Restriction_League.

that may have had an easy path toward citizenship may suddenly find itself barred due to popular sentiment. Though the 1965 Act is generally presented as having ended the national origins quota system, this is not quite true, despite the ending of the Asian exclusion. Numerical quotas for the different hemispheres, and for various preferences under national origins, remained in place; all that changed, essentially, was ending the official complete bar to Asian immigration.

As a result of the continued built-in anomalies, with allowances for Mexican immigration falling far short of the actual labor needs in agriculture and other labor-intensive industries, all of it worsened by Mexico's proximity, the contemporary "illegal immigration" problem was created and fueled. The 1965 Act enshrined family reunification, but this was partly a theoretical aspiration, since the numbers under the different preference systems (depending on relationship to U.S. citizens or permanent residents) were always inadequate to the needs, and because the system favored high-skilled over low-skilled immigrants, the other major innovation of the 1965 Act.

Over time, once the logic of the 1965 act took hold, it became true that increasingly greater proportions of immigrants arrived with a path to citizenship already in hand (such as the skilled H-1B workers who got a boost in early 1990s legislation), with families already in tow or on their way, while an increasingly smaller proportion of immigrants adjusted to permanent status after having arrived without inspection or having arrived on temporary visas. In other words, the 1965 Act had the (unintended) consequence of reducing pathways to citizenship for lower-skilled immigrants while reserving more and more of that privilege for higher-skilled immigrants.

The innovations of the 1990s neoliberal legislation.

These incongruities of the 1965 immigration act, our governing legislation to this day (in turn deriving from the root in the 1952 INA), manifested themselves in their most extreme form in a piece of legislation, the aforementioned 1996 IIRIRA, which provides the Trump administration with all the authority it needs for mass deportations without judicial review.

The 1996 law lumped exclusion and deportation proceedings into a common procedure called "removal," a sleight of hand making exclusion tantamount to inadmissibility, meaning that immigrants, even if they have been present on American soil for decades, can be considered not to be admitted, or present, and therefore deprived of all rights.

Anyone deportable, under the 1996 legislation that remains the law of the land, is handled according to the newly enshrined "removal proceedings," all of it limiting judicial overview to the point of nonexistence, reducing judges to rubber stampers. Asylum as we have known it ceased to exist in 1996, even if most Americans aren't aware of it, just as the Anti-Terrorism and Effective Death Penalty Act (AEDPA) of the same year vastly reduced judicial overview and imposed harsh penalties, and also allowed for secret evidence, a consistent feature of totalitarian regimes.

It is in these two destructive and interrelated laws, the culmination of more than a century of federal exclusionary policies, that we see the justification for the current rampant use of the term "criminal aliens." Making no distinction between crimes ranging from shoplifting to murder, all of which are categorized as "aggravated felonies," Congress has all but ended judicial review of removal orders and eliminated almost any possibility of relief from deportation. Moreover, "criminal aliens" (despite the surprise at Trump's explicit delineation of the policy) have been subject for more than twenty years to mandatory detention, pending final deportation.

While immigration agents are said to be enjoying new license under the Trump administration's leeway to detain "criminal aliens," in the wake of the 1996 law the then-INS's attitude was no different, as agents sought to gain credit by apprehending as many immigrants as possible. Prop. 187[1] in early 1990s California was the direct forerunner of the racially profiling ("show me your papers") SB 1070[2] law of Arizona in 2010, both of which in turn draw from the entire LPC discourse and potential denial of public services, including

---

[1] http://www.latimes.com/politics/la-me-on-politics-column-20170323-story.html.

[2] https://www.azleg.gov/legtext/49leg/2r/bills/sb1070s.pdf.

education, that have been staples of immigration discourse since federalization. Trump's current and envisioned executive orders merely continue this tendency.

The 1996 legislation in its entirety was unconstitutional; before 9/11, the courts had started chipping away at it bit by bit, but then the political environment made further erosion of its authority difficult.

For example, before 9/11, the Supreme Court, in *INS v. St. Cyr* (2001),[1] ruled that habeas corpus review remained intact despite Congress's laws with regard to "aggravated felons." Very significantly, in the 2001 case of *Zadvydas v. Davis*,[2] the question was about whether an immigrant could be indefinitely detained because no country was willing to take him. In the *Miller, Nguyen,* and *AADC* rulings preceding *Zadvydas,* the plenary power doctrine had been upheld again, yet the Court decided to take a different approach in *Zadvydas* and in *Ashcroft v. Ma*[3] (together known as *Zadvydas*), where Justice Stephen Breyer, along with O'Connor, Stevens, Souter, and Ginsburg, stated that "the Due Process Clause applies to all 'persons' within the United States, including aliens, whether their presence here is lawful, unlawful, temporary, or permanent."

Justice Breyer noted—and this is very important for the current controversy under Trump—that detention cannot be construed as a punishment because the criminal law context doesn't apply. The court noted its departure from *Shaughnessy v. Mezei*[4] (1953) in that the immigrant was already in the United States and his detention was subject to closer constitutional examination.

IIRIRA was passed in the midst of the 1990s moral panic, when terrorism wasn't the concern so much as immigrants siphoning off public benefits, with California's Prop. 187 going so far as to deem undocumented persons ineligible for *all* public services, including primary and secondary education, and basic health care. IIRIRA tried to move as far in this extreme direction as federal authority would

---

[1] https://www.oyez.org/cases/2000/00-767.

[2] https://supreme.justia.com/cases/federal/us/533/678/.

[3] https://scholar.google.com/scholar_case?case=17034221476555352999&q=ashcroft+v.+ma&hl=en&as_sdt=6,44&as_vis=1.

[4] https://supreme.justia.com/cases/federal/us/345/206/case.html.

allow it, holding that legal permanent residents were henceforth ineligible for any public assistance, since one of the leading (quite false) charges of the restrictionists has always been that immigrants are a drain on public resources, and a net negative from the fiscal standpoint.

IIRIRA created the category of "aggravated felonies," which included a vastly expanded list of "crimes," including passing bad checks, shoplifting, driving under the influence, minor drug possession, child abuse and neglect, and domestic violence, all of which became deportable offenses.

Not only that, but the aggravated felonies were made deportable retroactively; so for instance someone could have been in this country thirty, forty, or fifty years, and yet in an encounter with the authorities, if the past crime, for which a person had been duly punished already, came to light, then that person was deportable; indeed, under this law, untold numbers of people have been deported from the country, who had otherwise been law-abiding and had established families and businesses and community involvement here, because their past offense, which was not deportable when it was committed, became known.

In our criminal justice regime, defendants are pushed hard to accept plea bargains of guilt in return for reduced sentences, and millions of people have in the past taken advantage of it, not knowing that there would come a day when their plea bargain would be grounds for deportation. Though Trump captured attention with his first executive order, laying out that anyone can be deported who has committed a "chargeable" crime, this was merely full implementation of the 1996 law, nothing radically different.

As numerous immigration activists and scholars have documented, the options for judicial review, even for residents who have established roots in the community for decades, are severely limited, as judges' discretionary authority has been taken away. Defendants are forced to rely on claims that they will be tortured upon return to Latin American or African or Asian countries, with torture being interpreted in the narrowest possible terms; no amount of other hardship to the defendant of decades-long residency, and to his or her family in the United States, is taken under consideration.

IIRIRA also radically changed the refugee and asylum claims system, mandatorily putting asylum claimants in detention, dramatically reducing the possibility of any refugee or asylee gaining a path to legal status.

Imagine arriving from a country like Sudan or Iraq, after having already undergone torture or other human rights violations, and being put into the brutal private American detention system, or in faraway county jails with hardened criminals, because you're presumed to be a criminal before you've had a chance to prove your case, and with very little prospect of eventual success during the course of appeals. Mandatory detention for asylum seekers is indefinite and can last for years, despite several court rulings suggesting that indefinite detention is illegal.

Trump's extreme disrespect for refugees and asylum claimants is strongly rooted in existing legislation, and goes back to well-known instances in the 1950s, under the moral panic induced then by communism, with the courts upholding indefinite detention of refugees or returnees from Eastern Europe, even allowing them to be held on Ellis Island in permanent statelessness.

Immigration law restricts citizens' rights.

Whatever starts out as restricting the human rights of the most vulnerable amongst us—among them the undocumented, because the sword of deportation is always hanging above their heads—eventually gets extended to legal immigrants, and finally to citizens. The disciplinary state chooses immigrants as the first arena for implementation of human rights restrictions, knowing that the hue and cry will be limited, and will provide a sense of normalization about illegalities that would be more difficult if directly imposed on citizens.

It is not coincidental that when neoliberalism was consolidated in the mid-1990s, welfare, terrorism, and immigration legislation passed in the same year, and in fact bore very close resemblance to each other and were even overlapping.

The anti-immigrant legislation of 1996 provided precedents for the Bush regime's implementation of such unconstitutional measures as registration of Arabs and Muslims, which netted tens of thousands of immigrants who were deported for minor "crimes," as terrorism became completely intertwined with immigration, just as communist subversion had in earlier times.

Bush's attorney general John Ashcroft was throwing the widest possible sweep to net immigrants from Muslim countries in order to deport them for "chargeable" (if not actual) crimes, because there was no basis to prosecute them for terrorism; the administration was relying on the implied backing of the plenary power doctrine, as usual, to provide broad leeway in matters of national security. IIRIRA had already provided for sharply reduced judicial review for defendants charged with terrorism, so the defining authority was already there.

When civil liberties are abrogated for one group, this ends up being so for all groups. When due process and equal protection are constrained for immigrants, this eventually affects citizens as well. The farther the gap between immigrant and citizen, the more pressure it puts on citizenship to be downgraded to the status of the lowly immigrant, because citizenship becomes something so hyperlegal, so liberated from ordinary human rights discourse, that its traditional foundations, in ordinary notions of community and membership, become unsustainable.

To make sure that excessive law enforcement does not erode the rights of citizens, the gap between immigrant and citizen must be closed, not broadened.

Our historically abusive relationship with Mexico.

1994 is the year NAFTA was passed, and the contemporary immigration problem, in all its specific dimensions, first began manifesting, at precisely the same time.

At the heart of NAFTA's contradiction was the removal of barriers on capital, and the simultaneous installation of new barriers on immigration. At the same time as dramatic new push-and-pull factors were exerted on Mexico, leading to escalated immigration, the avenues for immigrants to gain citizenship were curtailed or ended. Mexico had pursued a protectionist, import substitution regime, like most developing countries, well into the 1970s, which led to opportunities for internal migration, from agriculture to industries; but NAFTA gave unfair subsidies to big American agriculture while putting unprecedented pressure on Mexican small farmers, and also weighed the scales against Mexican small industry.

All of this left no outlet valve for newly unemployed Mexicans than to migrate northward. In the past, this had not necessarily led to huge increases in the proportion of Mexicans compared to the overall immigrant population, but throughout the 1990s the border became less porous, the price of leaving the country and being unable to reenter more ominous, and the cycle of seasonal migration, which had been a staple of Mexican migration since the 1920s, was severely curtailed. It now became much more attractive for Mexican immigrants, instead of returning to Mexico from time to time, or even returning permanently, to put down roots in America, to start families and become part of communities and sever connections with Mexico.

So "illegal immigration" was an entirely self-created bureaucratic outcome, there was nothing inevitable about it, and the increase in "illegality" that came about had clear historical precedents.

The Bracero Program[1] had imported large numbers of Mexicans at mid-century, and Operation Wetback[2] (which Trump and his lieutenants fondly recite) was designed, in the 1950s, to satisfy xenophobic sentiment (the INS claimed having repatriated nearly a million and a half Mexicans), while continuing to meet American appetite for cheap labor; the deportees were often imported right back at the border, in a process called "drying out." In these mass deportation efforts, both in the 1930s and in the 1950s, untold numbers of American citizens of Mexican heritage were also sent back to Mexico; this process has its exact echoes in the deportations of the last two decades. Circularity was a sort of functionality, and it didn't lead to illegality, because whereas twenty eight million Mexicans entered the U.S. between the end of the Bracero program and the

---

[1] https://www.labor.ucla.edu/what-we-do/labor-studies/research-tools/the-bracero-program/.

[2] https://www.vox.com/2015/11/11/9714842/operation-wetback.

passage of the Immigration Reform and Control Act (IRCA) in 1986, nearly twenty four million left as well.

So the net result of NAFTA was to end the traditional circular flow of Mexican labor, advantage high-skilled over low-skilled labor while continuing to import large quantities of the latter, and for corporate America to countenance the lack of authorization while taking full advantage of a newly exploitable labor force—call it slave labor, if you will, with the same lack of human rights accorded to slaves.

To top it off, Mexican immigrants, over several decades of propaganda, have been firmly established in the popular imagination as excessively reliant on public assistance, or beholden to their native language, or prone to more crime than natives (all of which propositions are patently untrue), which helps to exert pressure on all immigrants and minorities, even native-born.

Our immigration policy is designed in such a way that Mexicans, particularly over the last two decades, have become concentrated in lower-skilled professions; this is very much a policy choice, but is it a policy we should countenance from a human rights point of view?

In effect, we have a growing stateless population buffering the native population from the worst effects of economic downturns, even as national policy prevents the full utilization of immigrants worldwide for economic growth; we want to keep labor dynamics within a narrow spectrum benefiting employers at a known level of certainty, meaning a certain kind of repression that disallows full dynamism.

"Comprehensive Immigration Reform" (CIR) in all its versions is a neoliberal boondoggle.

Ever since, and including, the 1986 IRCA, all comprehensive immigration reform (CIR) has sought to limit legal immigration, restrict the rights of existing immigrants, and make family unification and refugee and asylum claims more difficult; this is true of every single piece of CIR legislation, under various presidents, including George W. Bush's proposed 2006 and 2007 legislation, and Barack Obama's proposed 2013 legislation.

Republican senators have recently proposed new legislation to decrease legal immigration by half, among other things eliminating the preference for siblings of U.S. citizens and permanent residents (a standard tactic), but this is nothing new.[1] Senator Alan Simpson (who co-sponsored IRCA) and others who followed in his wake have desired to cut legal immigration by a third, a half, or even end it altogether, to take, as they call it, a "time-out," precisely as America did for forty years from 1925-1965; and the argument is precisely similar as in earlier instances, that we need time to assimilate the immigrants already here.

There is a permanent executive context for such CIR proposals to have traction. In the first four years of the Obama administration, deportations rose to four hundred thousand per year. While there is much hue and cry about Trump's executive orders giving license to local officials to go on fishing expeditions to discover illegal status, the peak of the cooperative agreements between ICE and state and local police, under the 287(g) section of the 1952 INA, was reached under the Obama administration, when thirty-five law enforcement agencies in eighteen states willingly participated.

All CIR consists of a three-pronged strategy: Increase enforcement, move to a guest worker program, and offer some limited legalization under extremely harsh conditions.

The amount of increase in Border Patrol numbers and resources, over a period of thirty years, is mind-boggling.[2] Yet during the 1990s and 2000s, despite such radical (militarized) Clinton-era innovations as Operation Gatekeeper[3] and Operation Hold the Line,[4] which forever altered the nature of the Mexican border, and despite the harsh post-9/11 detention regime imposed by George W. Bush (the number of federal detentions went up to forty thousand at any given time, where it stays today), immigration from Mexico did not decline;

---

[1] http://www.newsweek.com/republicans-immigration-government-shutdown-border-wall-dreamers-daca-786282.

[2] http://www.nnirr.org/drupal/border-militarization.

[3] https://www.foreignaffairs.com/reviews/capsule-review/2003-03-01/operation-gatekeeper-rise-illegal-alien-and-remaking-us-mexico.

[4] http://www.kvia.com/news/special-report-part-1-how-operation-hold-the-line-changed-the-border-20-years-ago/55694090.

in fact, there was a sharp escalation in the 1990s and well into the 2000s, until the economic collapse. The pressure exerted on Mexico due to neoliberal globalization was too great, and immigrants simply found more difficult terrain through which to enter, which caused more deaths in the desert but didn't really stem the numbers. Thus, CIR's first inclination is always to punish immigrants, even while realizing that making entry impossible is not realistic.

Before 9/11, President Bush was considering a vast expansion of guest workers, in talks with Mexican President Vicente Fox, which is supposed to have been the vaunted CIR initiative that got forestalled. In 2004, again, Bush's intention was to convert the entire undocumented population into guest workers without full human rights. Likewise, the 2006 and 2007 CIR bills (both of which were defeated in large part by the efforts of current attorney general Jeff Sessions, because ending immigration, not just curtailing it, is his goal) had guest workers as a key element, causing serious division between labor and immigrant advocates. The return that is promised, to compensate for the first two prongs of CIR, is always some form of legalization, but in reality, in the 2006, 2007, and 2013 Obama versions, very few immigrants would have qualified because of all the preconditions.

For the past thirty years CIR has always relied on a neoliberal discourse of crime, punishment, personal responsibility, and separation of the good from the bad that is a no-win situation for anyone interested in human rights.

To engage in the discourse of immigrants as worthy of welcome because they are economic contributors, or because we are a nation that rewards personal responsibility despite all odds, or because we should reward good behavior as opposed to bad, only leads to such dreadful outcomes as cleaving off a tiny slice of immigrants, the so-called Dreamers, who are said to have come here due to "no fault of their own," and to represent everything (getting through college despite every obstacle put in their path by the state, preserving unblemished police records despite being forced to grow up in high-crime neighborhoods) that we consider desirable about immigrants.

It all feeds into a neoliberal fantasy that we should take no part in, even if all the claims made about immigrants' contributions to the economy, not to mention sustaining the viability of retirement programs due to the otherwise aging population, are all true, and then some. That is not what immigration discourse should be about.

Trump is shrewd enough to deploy the Dreamers as a wedge issue in the immigration debate. He will hold on to canceling DACA (Deferred Action for Childhood Arrivals) until the last possible moment, in order to neutralize opposition from young, "law-abiding" immigrants who are expecting to maintain some sort of status to be allowed to live in this country.[1] Of course, they have no country "to go back to." But that is not any less true of someone else who may not have arrived, "through no fault of his or her own," into the country at a young age, but may have lived here for decades, and perhaps be an even greater contributor than the average so-called "Dreamer." This myth doesn't make any moral sense except under complete sway of the neoliberal discourse.

Though Trump's emphasis on criminalizing all immigrants is causing much consternation today, while CIR bills like the one in 2006 still get praise, Peter Schey of the Center for Human Rights and Constitutional Law noted at the time that it would have converted the majority of the undocumented into fugitives, since evading inspection would be made a "continuous" crime that would not end until the immigrant was "discovered."[2] Moreover, the 2006 Senate bill sought to overturn the Supreme Court's tentative grants of constitutional rights—such as limits on indefinite detention—and would have doubled down on the 1996 law by expanding aggravated felonies even further, stripped the courts of even more of their reviewing role pertaining to errors of enforcement, and forced asylum seekers to return to countries where they face torture and imprisonment.

The truth is that in all the years since the liberalization of immigration in 1965 we have not had a single piece of legislation that fully respects human rights, including the various concessions to

---

[1] https://www.usatoday.com/story/news/nation/2018/01/18/there-3-5-m-dreamers-and-most-may-face-nightmare/1042134001/.

[2] http://azdailysun.com/news/years-and-still-not-a-citizen/article_155aa097-b1c0-5b57-a8b3-2db7f0cf6c51.html.

refugees in the 1970s and 1980s, so nostalgia toward any recent administration or its proposed legislation is foolish.

The nexus between neoliberalism and the current immigration problem.

Trump has somewhat extended, in his initial executive orders, the definition of "criminal alien"—essentially, every immigrant is potentially a criminal alien, since there are many roadblocks on the pathway from temporary to permanent, or illegal to legal.

This is nothing new, however, as we've seen in the explanation of the 1996 law. The dreaded 2005 Sensenbrenner bill, HR 4437,[1] which caused the largest-ever immigration protests in our country, sought to criminalize illegal presence as a felony. Trump is not calling it a felony, yet, but simply assuming that it's a crime to be illegally present, even if one hasn't been issued with a deportation order.

The logic of neoliberal accountability inevitably leads to the criminalization of all immigrants—except some of those who enter as nonimmigrants yet with a predetermined path to citizenship, namely the skilled H-1B workers so popular with corporate America since around 1990.[2]

When Trump was saying during the campaign that he would deport all "criminal aliens," those who understand immigration knew that he wasn't talking about hardened criminals, but everyone unlucky enough to be present without legal status, and potentially even those with such status. Of course, being present without documentation is a civil issue, but it has been turned into an entirely criminal matter, after decades of restrictionist talk.

The LPC clause, as we have seen, has always been present, but it was not federalized at the onset of the republic, and it was not

---

[1] https://www.congress.gov/bill/109th-congress/house-bill/4437.

[2] But the Trump regime is taking aim at high-skilled immigration too: https://www.nytimes.com/2017/12/20/us/trump-immigration-slowdown.html?mtrref=www.google.com&gwh=EB3EA3F5208E7A3C5767FD3B 8226B91C&gwt=pay.

weaponized as a racist instrument to the extent that it is now. The 1996 law required U.S. citizen sponsors of parents or other relatives to sign affidavits of financial support, which made the sponsors accountable in courts of law should the sponsored falter and require public assistance; thus, if there were, for example, a health crisis for an elderly parent, the sponsor would be held responsible and face financial ruin. Such is our commitment to family unification, despite the rhetoric never having faded away in the most recent immigration debates.

These neoliberal measures are firmly rooted in three decades of panic at the state and federal level, with everyone desiring immigrants' economic and cultural contributions without expecting to be there for them in return. Mandatory detention, in unprecedented numbers, creates incentives for private prisons to push criminalization of immigration; in fact, the entire security complex is geared to lobby government for more criminalization, including that of asylum seekers and refugees.

If enough visas were made available for family unification or for work, there would be no "illegal" immigrants. But one shouldn't even have family in the United States or an employment offer as prerequisites to migrate. Ideally, immigration should be at least as self-regulating a function as taxation. Everyone who has a need to be in this country should be able to enter and file a self-declaration, and periodically file status updates. If one desires to stay in this country permanently, there should be as many pathways as possible so that one can fulfill one's potential rather than being forced to change one's life according to immigration law technicalities.

Persistent contradictions in immigration law.

Should constitutional rights apply to citizens only, or to all persons present in the United States? Do immigrants have the right to public services, including education, or are such rights limited to citizens? Is the power of the federal government unchecked when it comes to interpretation and administration of immigration laws? If yes, then why does the same calculus not apply to the states?

The Thirteenth, Fourteenth, and Fifteenth Amendments were designed to limit the power of the states over non-citizens, and guarantee rights to all "persons." The Fourteenth Amendment says that "no State…shall deprive any person of life, liberty, or property, without due process of law; nor deny to any person within its jurisdiction the equal protection of the laws." This prohibits incarceration without trial, as due process and equal protection of the law apply to all *persons*.

There is no doubt that the U.S. constitution is written with "persons" in mind, there is no assertion of someone having to be a citizen in order to be the recipient of rights. In liberal eras, the courts have upheld this position, whereas in more restrictionist political environments there has been difficulty holding on to the notion of personhood.

In *Matthews v. Diaz*[1] (1976), unfortunately the Supreme Court approved limits on the availability of federal medical insurance to lawful permanent residents, arguing that "the fact that Congress has provided some welfare benefits for citizens does not require it to provide like benefits for all aliens." But this was a federal issue, whereas the court, in the landmark *Plyler* case shortly thereafter, felt differently when it came to a Texas law barring education.

The issue of access to education illustrates the see-saw well. In the historic *Plyler v. Doe*[2] (1982) decision, the Supreme Court held that nonimmigrant students, regardless of status, have a right to K-12 schooling as long as others are being offered the same right. But the question arises, if higher education is as essential to a person's success in the United States as education up to high school, then why should higher education not fall under the same logic as *Plyler*? There is no logically consistent answer to this.

During the 1990s and 2000s, some states offered in-state tuition to undocumented students, while other, more restrictionist states (such as Arizona, Georgia, and Indiana) not only didn't offer in-state tuition but prohibited the enrollment of undocumented students in

---

[1] https://supreme.justia.com/cases/federal/us/426/67/case.html.
[2] https://www.americanimmigrationcouncil.org/research/plyler-v-doe-public-education-immigrant-students.

institutions of higher learning. From the point of view of the public good, to allow students to continue up to high school but then foreclose possibilities of equal access to education does not make sense.

As early as the 1880s, the courts held that individual states could not discriminate against immigrants on the matter of equal access to opportunities. It's unfortunate that in the increasing climate of xenophobia, until immigration was at last stalled in the 1920s, this doctrine did not get more of a chance to flourish. In *Truaux v. Raich*,[1] the Supreme Court held in 1915 that Arizona could not restrict the employment of aliens. Leading up to *Plyler*, in the post-civil rights euphoric mood of the early 1970s, the Supreme Court struck down Arizona and Pennsylvania statutes that discriminated against non-citizens for the grant of welfare benefits. And in *Graham v. Richardson*[2] in 1971, the Court held that a state could have "no special interest" in limiting to citizens the expenditure of tax revenues to which aliens had contributed.

Another consistent contradiction in immigration law is the issue of retroactivity, i.e., the punishment of crimes that were not upon commission held to be deportable. This could include participation in political organizations, such as the Communist party, which became a deportable crime in the 1950s, with the passage of the Internal Security Act of 1950, or deportation on the basis of contribution to charities that were looked upon with favor in the 1990s but after 9/11 came under the broad umbrella of terrorism.

The 1996 law, as noted, is the most egregious offender in this regard, as it reclassifies numerous petty transgressions, everything from shoplifting to passing a bad check, as "aggravated felonies" worthy of deportation regardless of the length of stay and the family and community ties of the immigrant.

The courts have never satisfactorily resolved if immigrants are persons, which makes all the difference in the world because the constitution clearly applies to persons, not citizens only.

---

[1] https://supreme.justia.com/cases/federal/us/239/33/.

[2] https://www.oyez.org/cases/1970/609.

If this reminds us of the category of African Americans as not being fully persons at one time, then it should; the present impasse, which has really been going on since the 1880s, is one of the last remaining major hurdles in the realization of the American constitution. Because of the indecision, the courts have had a mixed history on membership versus exclusion, often arriving at quite inconsistent decisions. There are both plenty of good and bad precedents for legal doctrine to draw on in the future.

For example, *Gonzales v. City of Peoria*[1] (1983) curtailed the powers of local police to enforce immigration laws unless there was already a federally authorized criminal investigation in progress. But during the 1990s and 2000s, in such decisions as *United States v. Vasquez Alvarez*[2] (1999) and *United States v. Santana-Garcia*[3] (2001), the effect of the *Gonzalez* precedent was weakened as local police were given broad discretionary powers.

The problem with the plenary power doctrine.

To the extent that the Trump administration is likely to get away with mass deportations, it is the plenary power doctrine, i.e., the presumption of unlimited executive authority on matters of immigration, that will be the doctrinal support. But here too the picture is not one-sided or consistent: There have been decisions both supportive and skeptical of the plenary power doctrine, depending on the political climate of the moment. The courts have a mixed history on this.

As mentioned earlier, the plenary power doctrine originates in the Supreme Court's 1889 decision in *Chae Chin Ping v. United States*, where *Chae* was a U.S. resident who left for China for a visit but was denied re-entry because the Chinese Exclusion Act was passed in the meantime.

The *Chae* ruling was extended in *Fong Yue Ting v. United States*[4] shortly thereafter (1893), where the court upheld the deportation of

---

[1] https://openjurist.org/722/f2d/468/gonzales-v-city-of-peoria.
[2] http://caselaw.findlaw.com/us-10th-circuit/1317188.html.
[3] http://caselaw.findlaw.com/us-10th-circuit/1003211.html.

Fong because he could not, according to the government, produce a "credible white witness" to support his claim of residency. In Fong, the court held that "the right to exclude or to expel all aliens, or any class of aliens…[is] an inherent and inalienable right of every sovereign and independent nation, essential to its safety, its independence and its welfare….[and is] absolute and unqualified."

Around the same time, however, another important decision, *Yick Wo v. Hopkins*,[1] struck down a San Francisco ordinance that discriminated against the Chinese in their operation of laundries; when it came to local enforcement, the court felt that the Fourteenth Amendment's equal protection clause applied.

In *Harisiades v. Shaugnessy*[2] (1952), which allowed the deportation of three immigrants, former Communist Party members, Justice Frankfurter held that "The conditions for entry of every alien, the particular classes of aliens that shall be denied entry altogether, the basis for determining such classifications, the right to terminate hospitality to aliens, the grounds on which such determination shall be based, have been recognized as matters solely for the responsibility of the Congress and wholly outside the power of this Court to control." This repugnant doctrine has been extended over the last seventy years to permanent residents.

Two other notorious cases supporting ideological exclusion give Trump everything he needs to enforce a wider Muslim ban, including the resident population.

In *Knauff v. Shaughnessy*[3] (1950), the Supreme Court permitted the exclusion of Ellen Knauff, the non-citizen wife of a U.S. citizen, without a hearing, based entirely on confidential information. The court held that "The exclusion of aliens is a fundamental act of sovereignty. The right to do so stems not from legislative power alone but is inherent in the executive power to control the foreign affairs of the nation."

---

[4] https://supreme.justia.com/cases/federal/us/149/698/case.html.
[1] https://www.oyez.org/cases/1850-1900/118us356.
[2] https://www.quimbee.com/cases/harisiades-v-shaughnessy.
[3] https://aclu.procon.org/view.resource.php?resourceID=000370.

As for *Shaughnessy v. Mezei*[1] (1953), Ignatz Mezei had lived in this country from 1923 to 1948, but was prevented re-entry from Romania and detained at Ellis Island. The Supreme Court upheld his detention even though no country was willing to take him, leading to the possibility of indefinite detention.

On the other hand, going as far back as Secretary of State Elihu Root's opinion, in 1910, that there should be an "international minimum standard" for aliens, the Court has also gone in the other direction.

In *Whitfield v. Hanges*,[2] the Supreme Court held in 1915 that "an alien, as well as a citizen, is protected by the prohibition of deprivation of life, liberty, or property without due process and the equal protection of its laws. This principle is universal. It applies to all persons within the territorial jurisdiction of the United States without regard to any differences of race, or color or of nationality."

Likewise, in *Colyer v. Skeffington*,[3] a federal court held in 1920 that "aliens have constitutional rights. The Fourth, Fifth, Sixth, and Fourteenth Amendments are not limited in their application to citizens. They apply generally to all persons, within the jurisdiction of the United States."

So the plenary power doctrine has never been absolute; it comes into play at restrictionist moments, and is then presented as singularly relevant, but that is not the case. If we are to resolve the immigration dilemma, the legislature has to take the initiative by passing laws enshrining human rights for all immigrants, regardless of status or length of stay, laws that would be as momentous as the civil rights or voting rights acts.

The focus, for activists and thinkers, should shift from legalizing only some of the people, provided stringent neoliberal conditions of personal responsibility are met—I mean a small subset of the young undocumented population called the Dreamers—to demanding full human rights, and an end to detention following the withholding of

---

[1] http://www.lawschoolcasebriefs.net/2013/11/shaughnessy-v-united-states-ex-rel.html.

[2] https://case-law.vlex.com/vid/222-f-745-8th-595314818.

[3] https://case-law.vlex.com/vid/265-f-17-d-594220294.

human rights, for all persons in the U.S. Legalization per se should *not* be the focus, but the extension of human rights.

The recent scare,[1] in leaked DHS memos, that the National Guard would be at the service of states enforcing mass deportation, is beside the point. The Guard may or may not be used, we are past that concern. Even without the use of the military, which was the case during the climax of Operation Wetback, far greater numbers of immigrants are being administratively removed each year.[2] Such a vast machinery for removal of hundreds of thousands of persons each year with ties to the community bears comparison with the removal of Native Americans and with the forced displacement of West Africans as slaves.

Immigrants should have the same legal rights as everyone else.

All the categories deployed today in immigration discourse—refugee/immigrant/non-immigrant—are mythical, and their continued usage does not serve the cause of human rights.

With the widespread prevalence of mixed-status families, the legal/illegal definition becomes ridiculous. A parent may have arrived illegally or lost status twenty or thirty years ago, but may have children who were born here and are by definition U.S. citizens; at some point, should the children be able to sponsor the parent? And if that possibility is open, then is the parent immigrant an "illegal" person?

As noted already, most who become legal in the United States these days arrive with non-immigrant visas that already put them on the path to citizenship, whereas the same path is not open to others. In this context, "entering without inspection," an established category in immigration, makes as little sense as the existing preferences in the legal immigration system, which give priority to immigrants who may

---

[1] https://www.theguardian.com/us-news/2017/feb/17/trump-immigration-roundup-national-guard.

[2] http://abcnews.go.com/Politics/obamas-deportation-policy-numbers/story?id=41715661.

have had nothing to do with the United States, compared to those who may already have spent most of their lives here.

A Canadian-style merit-based points system (mentioned by Trump in his first speech to congress), if deployed in the United States, is likely to become a pure neoliberal instrumentality, merely extending the already existing biases inherent in the H-1B system toward high-skilled professionals to the entire immigrant population. The goal, for a human rights immigration regime, should be get away from preferences of any sort.

Much of the "illegality" stems from the unreasonable years-long backlog for those who are "in line"—up to twenty years for certain immigrant family members. Will people wait out the bulk of their productive lives before joining family members in the United States? If there were zero backlog, and such a state would easily be possible with self-entry and self-exit, then by definition the problem of illegality would cease to exist. If we couldn't file tax returns for twenty years, our earnings in the meantime would become "illegal" and subject to being seized, but would that be a fair system?

On the other end of the spectrum from high-skilled immigrants, what is a refugee? When do we explicitly create them, when are we not directly responsible, and do we have a special responsibility for the former?

Immigration law since the end of World War II, once the mistake about not letting in Jews fleeing the Holocaust was realized, has been littered with one inconsistent exception after another when it comes to refugees. Cubans have always received preferential treatment, while Haitians get the exact opposite of the treatment meted out to our favorite (light-skinned) Caribbean neighbors.[1] If a Cuban arrived on U.S. shores (at least until the 1980 Mariel boatlift, when Castro released Cuban prisoners and caused great consternation) he or she was automatically on the path to legality, whereas Haitians fleeing political turmoil, often worsened by our own interventions, have been forcefully turned away in shows of brutality.[2]

---

[1] http://www.coha.org/disparities-in-u-s-immigration-policy-toward-haiti-and-cuba-a-legacy-to-be-continued/.

[2] http://edition.cnn.com/2002/LAW/10/30/immigration.rules/index.html.

In many parts of the world the existence of refugees has been, for seventy-plus years, the direct consequence of our interventions: Vietnam, Cambodia, Afghanistan, Iran, El Salvador, Guatemala, and Honduras are a few examples, and most recently the refugees caused by our intervention in Syria. Sometimes we have taken special responsibility toward refugees created by our actions, while at other times we have outright refused them acceptance, as in the case of Iran, and now increasingly in the case of Syria. We have taken in refugees from Central America during the 1980s and 1990s, granted them temporary status, then threatened to withdraw such status, depending on the political winds.

Ultimately, the concept of refugee has become fatally compromised, and serves at this point only to drive a wedge between refugees and other immigrants, as though there were a line that could be drawn between economic and political motivations for immigration. Are political refugees not economic migrants? Are economic migrants not political refugees?

Similarly, the border is the reified concept that has most gotten out of control because of the political meanings invested in it. There can be no rational solution for immigration until we do away with the concept of the border.

Whereas Trump wants to erect a wall—this too has been a constant in American political mythology, going back a hundred years, and manifesting either as a fence or a wall, depending on the degree of restrictionism—at the Mexican border, most nonimmigrants fly into the country and are either on a path to citizenship or not; increasingly, the flight into the country is a binary situation, as options to adjust status have been reduced.

The border extends internally and infinitely, policing employers, schools, hospitals, welfare centers, day labor sites, driver's license offices, social security offices, and roads and highways: The only solution, to end the relentlessly growing idea of the border, is to end sanctions on employers and return instead to human rights for all workers. In fact, the restriction of workers' rights and the restriction of immigrant rights have gone hand in hand and are interdependent, as trade unions have started to recognize for the last thirty years.

Any guest worker program trades on the aberrations of the "border," and replicates new systems of policing and repression, and should be no part of a humanistic immigration initiative; it further consolidates the existing class biases in the immigration system. A "guest worker" is supposed to be one who works in agriculture or manual occupations, but a professional H1-B engineer is not a "guest worker," though he or she also arrives with temporary status; we need not harden such inconsistencies by giving any credibility to guest worker programs. Germany faced a crisis in the 1980s, with many Turkish workers who had been imported as guest workers, though German laws didn't allow them access to citizenship; that situation has since been corrected, but it is never one to promote.

If we were serious about ending the repressive effects of the border, then we would reconsider so-called 'free trade" agreements, which are really nothing but formalized concessions to various corporate monopolies, and which are the direct cause of massive displacement in Mexico and Central America.

We would end the ultimately dehumanizing practice of detention, by shutting down all detention centers, ending all roadblocks, checkpoints, and raids, and getting private business out of immigration enforcement, not by way of making it a federal monopoly, but by ending the concept altogether.

What, exactly, at this point is the border supposed to keep out?

Since the economic crisis and our intensifying human rights violations, net immigration from Mexico has been negative; no doubt, if circular flows were allowed as in the past, net immigration would have fallen dramatically in the negative, as many immigrants would have returned home. If we want to decrease immigration, if that is even the goal, then we should abolish the border as a concept. Many will want to leave, as was true until the 1920s, many will return to their countries carrying the seeds of American ideals, in a healthy two-way exchange of migration.

In short, the myth of the Dreamer, the privileging of the length of stay, and the social construction of the good versus the bad immigrant are all completely arbitrary designations that do not help a human rights discourse. It is neoliberal inhumanity to construct the myth of the young, physically vigorous, super-loyal, energetic, unresentful

Dreamer, grateful and gracious to the core, while excluding from immigrant mythology the disabled, older people, learners and caregivers, artists and creative people, and those who cannot be employed in the professions and activities neoliberalism emphasizes.

A vision for the future.

Just as states such as Arizona, Alabama, Georgia and others have taken restrictionist action in recent years, more progressive states such as California (which has done a hundred and eighty-degree turnaround since the days of Prop. 187) or those in the Pacific Northwest or Northeast or New England should take dramatic action in the opposite direction, by way of granting full constitutional rights to immigrants, including rights to all public services available to anyone else.

The situation before the federalization of immigration before the 1880s was quite like this, with states varying in their level of acceptance toward immigrants. Why should immigration fall under federal jurisdiction only? If there are states in the south and southwest that want to take away human rights, then other states in the northeast or northwest can step in to correct the imbalance and provide a counterweight for national discourse.[1]

The sanctuary concept so much under discussion at the moment shouldn't just be limited to protection from ICE raids, but extend to the idea of states granting full human rights to all persons. Whereas the federal government is making the lives of immigrants as difficult as possible (seeking "self-deportation," or "voluntary departure"), progressive states could try to make their lives as comfortable as possible. The Supreme Court has in recent years shown more deference to the states in general, under the commerce clause and the enforcement of civil rights laws under the Fourteenth Amendment, and perhaps something like that was in play when the lower courts ruled in favor of states bringing suits against Trump's travel ban.

One of the most instructive developments in immigration is the recent history of Iowa, which took the initiative to welcome

---

[1] http://blog.cyrusmehta.com/2015/01/the-laboratories-of-democracy-state-initiative-and-promotion-of-immigration-reform.html.

immigrants in the years before 9/11 in a truly radical manner; correctly, Governor Ted Strickland felt that immigration was the only way to rescue the flagging Midwestern economies. Yet restrictionists put pressure on the state of Iowa to backtrack, and soon—especially after 9/11—Iowa slid all the way to becoming a state where well-publicized raids made it lose all of its immigrant-friendly luster.

All over the Midwest, in towns that had not previously known Latino immigration, the native white population has rebelled over the last twenty years, pressing for mass arrests and deportations even if it meant that the towns in question would suffer irreversible decline, as has happened in many cases. The famous 2008 Pottsville raid, which destroyed a kosher meatpacking plant, put the kibosh on Iowa's stand as an immigrant-friendly state; the Latino workers arrested were only given the choice, en masse, of pleading to either lesser or greater felony charges, the lesser charge carrying a mandatory six-month detention, which every immigrant took.[1]

But Iowa is not every state, and outside pressure groups, such as the organizations operating under the racist FAIR umbrella, are not equally potent everywhere. Nothing could move immigration discourse in the correct direction so much as a state like California passing a full-fledged anti-SB 1070 (the racist Arizona law) to grant complete human rights to all persons present in California, regardless of status.

Moving beyond that, the long-term vision—just as is true of federal intervention in marriage or sexuality or the use of drugs or crime and rehabilitation in general—should be *no immigration laws*. Immigration should be decriminalized. By definition, the federal bureaucracy since 1880s has existed to enforce exclusion of various sorts, which is usually politically motivated, irrational when it comes to the public good, and counterproductive at the economic, philosophical, and moral levels.

Immigration should become a purely voluntary event, and the act of entering the United States and staying within the territory should be no more cumbersome than it is to file a tax return today. Persons

---

[1] http://www.thegazette.com/subject/news/iowas-hometown-to-the-world-20170326.

can voluntarily indicate, to the state and locality in question, their intention to stay, and there should be a transparent mechanism for describing the equities they start accumulating in the community.

Certainly, any person present in the United States should be able to vote, which would mean that the existing anomaly of "taxation without representation" (which is true of all immigrants until they become citizens, contributing huge amounts to the public coffers without getting much in return) would finally cease to exist. What if an enlightened person has been in the United States for only six months: Should they not be allowed to vote? And if they are, should there even be a distinction between local and national elections?

There is no rational basis, in the end, to deprive anyone present of the right to vote. Those who have been here any length of time are already denizens, who should have equal access to all public services and duties, contradicting our collective fantasies of a border that keeps out the undeserving other.

In the end there should be no separation between immigration and criminal law. Immigration is a civil matter, and it should remain so, even if the trend recently has been otherwise.

As pointed out earlier, immigration is treated for all intents and purposes as a criminal matter, though the fiction is preserved that it is a civil matter. Therefore, the accused immigrant suffers from all the disabilities of the criminal justice system without having any of its rights, because of that fiction. There should be no such thing as being prosecuted, in a criminal manner, including being detained, for an immigration matter. If an immigrant commits a crime, he or she should be prosecuted as a criminal (not as a criminal immigrant), just like anyone else.

It is only a completely free movement of people, with open borders, or rather the end of borders as such, that will eliminate the human rights crisis that we are currently facing. To move in that direction would be as significant as our abolition of the concept of slavery after the Civil War, with the same national and worldwide repercussions for liberty.

------

[1] https://jacksonlee.house.gov/media-center/press-releases/congresswoman-sheila-jackson-lee-re-introduces-the-save-america.

Migration is a universal human right. Congresswoman Sheila Jackson Lee's proposed 2005 Save America Comprehensive Immigration Act[1] took some steps in this direction by restoring some civil and due process rights stripped away in 1996, but it was only a small beginning, and of course it went nowhere in the climate of emphasizing guest workers.

Ultimately citizenship should return to what it was for a hundred years after the beginning of our republic, not an instrument of empire, of unfair privileges enforced against certain deprived and targeted populations, but a right based on personhood and deriving from democratic membership, accessible to everyone.

Citizenship should be stripped of the power to discriminate, along with the end of rabid nationalism. If every person present in the United States had exactly the same rights, citizenship would become less important (as it was, in some ways, before the 1996 law, when many chose not to naturalize despite being present for decades).

In the end, this analysis shows that illegality is a purely technical or administrative issue which has been turned into criminality; it is a postmodern version of imagined criminality, like the one-drop rule, or any of the historic buttresses of pure racism. We are inhabiting— and Trump's proposals only formalize the idea—a postmodern slave economy, under cover of a free-trade (NAFTA-oriented) regime.

We have moved very rapidly, under Clinton-Bush-Obama and now Trump, in the direction of endowing citizenship with a nationalist prowess that has become almost indistinguishable from white supremacy. If we retort to this white nationalism by way of economic arguments for immigration (which are certainly true and valid on their face), then we become apologists for the existing unfair economy, because that is what we are really defending.

The right to exclusion, which is generally justified as a national sovereignty's right to prevent excessive numbers, is actually always racist. There is no such thing as "excessive" numbers, it is always national sentiment that arises in response to immigrants who look and sound different than us, at least in the beginning. All the arguments one has heard in the last thirty-five years of active restrictionism about immigrants' impact on jobs, housing, crime, the environment, and the culture have no basis in reality, as numerous empirical exercises have proved.

If there were no border controls, studies in the 1980s showed that world economic output would double; research in the 2000s suggested even greater gains for the world economy. In essence, immigration policy, particularly in the United States, has been a brake on economic, and therefore cultural, dynamism, ever since its inception.

If we are currently in the midst of a nationalist fervor that threatens our democracy at the core, at least partly it is because we have immigrants without legislative representation, and because we preserve a permanent segment of the population without human rights; the overall effect on democratic health is no different than in the days of slavery, it makes of citizenship a flesh and blood monster while reducing its beneficial democratic impact.

Just as slaves were nonpersons, we notice that Trump resorts exclusively to speaking of "criminal aliens," having expanded the definition of crime to presence and every activity an immigrant is likely to pursue, so that the two terms, criminal and alien, have become indistinguishable. To return to justice in our immigration laws, these two categories, criminality and alienage, must be radically separated.

The Supreme Court, in its better moments, has acknowledged that "deportation may result in the loss of all that makes life worth living" (*Bridges v. Wixon*, 1945).[1] This harshest of all punishments must be eliminated, it is as cruel as separating the families of slaves from each other.

In just the decade following the 1996 legislation, the U.S. government detained and deported 1.6 million immigrants, and forced *twelve million voluntary departures*. In the first six months of 2011, ICE deported more than forty-six thousand parents with at least one U.S. citizen child; and we are afraid of Trump's deportation force? At what numerical scale are we allowed to describe this as genocide? There need not be the National Guard on the streets when

---

[1] http://caselaw.findlaw.com/us-supreme-court/326/135.html.

the tasks can be done administratively; the 2005 REAL ID Act, for example, stripped immigrants of the right to habeas corpus.

More than eighty thousand workers—and this number should grow exponentially under Trump—are already employed in what has been called the "border-industrial complex"; the amount of technology deployed (nearly twenty thousand vehicles) is reminiscent of war, while the fence itself already extends to every feasible part of the border. The number of border patrol agents has gone up from thirty-five hundred in 1992 to more than twenty thousand today, with Trump wishing to add ten thousand more.

Such figures, especially in light of the fact that during the 1990s the numbers of migrants didn't decrease, suggest that it is not about a rational control of borders but an implementation of a supremacist fantasy of impermeable borders. Despite all the border controls of the 1990s, the number of immigrants coming across the southern border was roughly comparable—four hundred thousand or more each year—to the number that we were importing during the Bracero program.

The entire political discourse that holds out immigrants as worthy of compassion because they do the dirty work no Americans would want to do, or because they feed and nurse us and build our houses and grow our food, is repellant in the extreme; it feeds into a mentality that prevents human rights from being extended to all persons.

We do not say of human beings that they deserve human rights because they are of utility to others; human beings are entitled to rights despite doing things that go against our notions of the good or virtuous. Short of this realization, we will remain a barbaric society with the mentality of slave-owners. Right-wing discourse in this country has slowly converted constitutional rights into privileges; as we participate in this discourse for immigrants, all such rights, from freedom of speech and association to equal protection, ultimately get abridged for citizens as well.

Imagine a country where an upstanding citizen with decades of contribution to our community suddenly gets caught up in the legal crosshairs; the judge has no right to consider a pardon, regardless of the immigrant's status in the community since the commission of the original transgression, which can be as minor as drunk driving; furthermore, the immigrant must remain in detention until the final order of deportation. Is that a country we want to live in? Will such abuse be limited to immigrants?

As I said at the beginning, there is a mistaken belief that there exists a line to get legal status—there is no such thing as a line to get into!—and that once a person marries a U.S. citizen or has U.S. citizen children there are some constitutional rights attached with it. Nothing could be further from the truth. Comprehensive immigration reform as we know it is simply another name for further delegalization, without the possibility of pardon or parole, and it should be no part of advocacy discourse.

About the Author

Anis Shivani is a fiction writer, poet, literary critic, and political analyst living in Houston, Texas. His critically acclaimed books include *Anatolia and Other Stories*, *The Fifth Lash and Other Stories*, *Karachi Raj: A Novel*, *My Tranquil War and Other Poems*, *Whatever Speaks on Behalf of Hashish: Poems*, *Soraya: Sonnets*, *The Moon Blooms in Occupied Hours: Poems*, *Against the Workshop: Provocations, Polemics, Controversies*, and *Literary Writing in the Twenty-First Century: Conversations*. His work appears widely in such journals as the *Yale Review*, *Georgia Review*, *Southwest Review*, *Boston Review*, *Threepenny Review*, *Michigan Quarterly Review*, *Antioch Review*, *Black Warrior Review*, *Western Humanities Review*, *Boulevard*, *Pleiades*, *AGNI*, *Fence*, *Denver Quarterly*, *Volt*, *Subtropics*, *New Letters*, *Times Literary Supplement*, *London Magazine*, *Cambridge Quarterly*, *Contemporary Review*, *Meanjin*, *Fiddlehead*, *Dalhousie Review*, *Antigonish Review*, and elsewhere. He has also written for many magazines and newspapers including *Salon*, *Daily Beast*, *AlterNet*, *CommonDreams*, *Counterpunch*, *Truthout*, *Huffington Post*, *Texas Observer*, *In These Times*, *Boston Globe*, *San Francisco Chronicle*, *Kansas City Star*, *Pittsburgh Post-Gazette*, *Baltimore Sun*, *Charlotte Observer*, *Austin American-Statesman*, and elsewhere. He is the winner of a Pushcart Prize, and a graduate of Harvard University.